THE ASSASSINATION
of
MARY MAGDALENE

Julian Doyle

Why through the whole of history has the Church made such a vicious and concerted character assassination on one of the most important persons in the Christian Bible?

Taking Luke's description of the Magdalene:

*'Mary Magdalene, out of whom had
come seven demons.' (Luke 8)*

From this one sentence the Church decided that Mary Magdalene was, not only a sinner and a prostitute, but in AD 591 Pope Gregory declared the *'seven demons'* were in fact the seven deadly sins of pride, envy, gluttony, greed, lust, sloth and wrath and heaped all these seven sins on to her, on top of prostitution. So this infallible Pope had pronounced Mary Magdalene to be a fat, greedy, lazy, jealous, angry prostitute! You can see that the church shows no restraint when it comes to assassinating the character of Mary Magdalene.

Why?

COVER: MARY MAGDALENE - Caravaggio

To Mary Magdalene
Apostle to the Apostles

Introduction

The concerted character assassination of Mary Magdalene has puzzled many through the ages. Some believe it was to conceal a marriage between Jesus and the Magdalene but whether there was a marriage or even a sexual relationship between the two, this is actually not the reason for these vicious attacks on her. If there had been a marriage it would not change one word of the Gospels, as they neither say Jesus was married or that he was not. They are silent on the issue.

But the reason for the attack is much more complex and is nothing to do with events while Jesus was alive. It is actually to do with what happened to the Magdalene after His death and they are to conceal a truth that any serious investigation of the Magdalene would unravel. A truth that was so well known in the South of France that a crusade was launched against the area. It began with an attack on July 22, 1209 on the town of Beziers where the doors of the church of St. Mary Magdalene were broken down and the refugees from the surrounding area were dragged out and slaughtered. This ended in 7,000 deaths including women and children. Thousands of people were mutilated and killed. Prisoners were blinded, dragged behind horses and used for target practice. Arnaud wrote to Pope Innocent III that 20,000 of these Christians were put to sword, regardless of rank, age or sex. I would ask you to note that the church in Beziers that was attacked was called Saint Mary Magdalene's but the Church of Rome did not make the

Magdalene a Saint for another seven hundred and fifty years. Furthermore the attack was launched on 22nd July, which was Mary Magdalene' feast day! So these innocent people clearly held Mary Magdalene in high esteem and it cost them their lives.

We can be sure that the church of Rome was making a concerted effort not only to destroy the reputation of the Magdalene, but to destroy all knowledge of the real story of this important woman that was held in high esteem the Languedoc.

What appears to have happened after these attacks in France was that the information was forced underground but can be glimpsed in rituals of initiation in secretive organizations. For instance in the council of Troyes the most curious of oaths was imposed on the Templar Knights:

'Obedience to Bethany, the castle of Mary and Martha'

What possible reason could an order of 'warrior' monks, formed to protect pilgrims on the roads in the Holy Land, be swearing allegiance to the building, which housed the Magdalene and her sister Martha? (we will deal with the odd invention of Mary of Bethany later)

A hundred years after the attack on Beziers and the Languedoc the Templar organization was also attacked as heretical and their leader, Jacques de Molay, was tied to a stake erected on the small Isle des Juifs in the Seine to be roasted alive. Jacques DeMolay refused all offers of pardon if he retracted his beliefs, and as the bones of his toes blackened and fell onto the hot coals he bore his torment with a composure, that won for him the reputation of a martyr.

What were those beliefs that he was prepared to suffer and die for? And what element of them revolved around the building in Bethany and the family who lived there that he had sworn allegiance to? And are these beliefs still with us somewhere? Here is a letter sent by Louis Fouquet to his brother Nicholas Fouquet after a meeting in Rome with the enigmatic painter Poussin.

'He and I discussed certain things, which I shall with ease be able to explain to you in detail – things which will give you, through Monsieur Poussin, advantages which even kings would have great pains to draw from him, and which, according to him, it is possible that nobody else will ever rediscover in the centuries to come.' (Letter: Louis Fouquet)

Fouquet was subsequently arrested and imprisoned being held strictly incommunicado for the rest of his life. Even the jailers were forbidden to talk to him. Some historians regard him as a possible candidate for the 'man in the iron mask'. Fouquet's correspondence was confiscated by King Louis XIV, who inspected them personally. The King went on to obtain Poussin's arcane painting of 'Les Bergers d'Arcadia', which he kept in his private apartments in Versailles.

What is revealed when one puts together the real story of the Magdalene is, without doubt, what Poussin thought, *"Nobody else will ever rediscover in the centuries to come.'*

Chapter One

THE WITNESSES

There are four witnesses to the life and death of Jesus, and these four, Matthew, Mark, Luke and John are the only, near contemporary source of information, we have about Mary Magdalene. You may think you know the story told in these four Gospels but you don't! What you know is a pic-and-mix version and I could take the Gospels and pic-and-mix a totally different story. But not only is it a pic-and-mix but some parts of the story you know are not even in the Gospels! Before I give you an example, you need to get to know these four witnesses as separate people so you can judge their evidence.

It is reported by several early church fathers that, Mark was an associate of Peter and wrote his Gospel in Rome.

"Mark, the disciple and interpreter of Peter did hand down to us what had been preached by Peter." (Irenaeus)

Luke on the other hand traveled with Paul.

'Luke the companion of Paul, recorded in a book the Gospel preached by him.' (Irenaeus)

It is vital to note that like Paul, Luke never knew Jesus, which he admits when opening his Gospel.

'Many have undertaken to draw up an account of the things that have been fulfilled just as they were handed down to us... I myself have carefully investigated everything, and have decided to write an orderly account for you, most excellent Theophilus.' (Luke 1)

So clearly, Luke has no personal information concerning Jesus, his evidence is all hearsay, so actually in a court of law his testimony would be ruled out. Luke and Matthew appear to follow Mark's story so these three Gospels are lumped together and called the synoptic Gospels, from the Latin, which means 'seen with one eye.' These synoptic Gospels, Mark, Luke and Matthew tell many of the same stories, often in the same words, frequently following the same order. They in fact, were the original Bible and John was added later.

'Afterwards, John, the disciple of the Lord, who also had leaned upon His breast, did himself publish a Gospel.' (Irenaeus)

Now I have suggested that you don't really know what is in the Gospels and that some of the story you know is actually not even in those Gospels. I assume you considered that rather arrogant, so I better give you an example. You know the famous story of Jesus triumphal entry into Jerusalem riding on a donkey, the streets filled by cheering crowds who shout Hosannas and lay palm leaves before him on the road. The image appears in every picture book and movie.

It is celebrated as Palm Sunday in the Christian calendar. Then when Jesus arrives at the Temple he takes a cord and drove all from the Temple court,

'scattering the coins of the money changers and overturned their tables.' (John 2:15)

You have seen it in every Biblical film of Passion Week. In fact Academics have tried to understand why the Jerusalem crowds who acclaim Jesus on this day, end up demanding his crucifixion by the end of the week. Others have claimed Jesus must have been a popular revolutionary. But the problem is that all this, much discussed Triumphal entry is actually, not in the Gospels. Yes you heard that right, it is not in any of the four Gospels. Here for instance is Mark's account:

'Jesus entered Jerusalem and went into the temple courts. He looked around at everything, but since it was already late, he went out to Bethany with the Twelve.' (Mark 11:11)

Surprised? I certainly was. Where are the crowds shouting Hosannas? Where are the moneychangers? Where are the Roman soldiers ready to arrest this liberator? Where is the Triumphal entry that is so discussed by academics? So this witness clearly states, there is no triumphal entry in to Jerusalem. Perhaps it is in Luke:

'They brought the colt to Jesus, threw their cloaks on it and put Jesus on it. As he went along, people spread their cloaks on the road. When he came near the place where the road goes down the Mount of Olives, the whole crowd of disciples began joyfully to praise God in loud voices for all the miracles they had seen: "Blessed is the king who comes in the name of the Lord!" (Luke 19:35)

So in Luke, it is the disciples who are the crowd praising God. They are the ones who can cheer *'for all the miracles they had seen'* not the residents of Jerusalem. We are talking about at least twelve disciples, surrounding Jesus on the donkey. Is this the crowd who are making all the noise when he gets on the donkey in Bethany?

So this is a more accurate representation, not in the streets but a mile and a half away in Bethany. And in fact when this crowd of disciples enter Jerusalem Matthew says:

"When Jesus entered Jerusalem, the whole city was stirred and asked, "Who is this?" (Matthew 21:10)

So in this Gospel the population of Jerusalem are not cheering the *'miracles they had seen'*, they are just totally baffled as to, who this person is who comes riding into their town surrounded by twelve noisy disciples.

In the modern telling of the story all these contradictions are ignored and a Triumphal entry is invented with cheering crowds in the streets of Jerusalem followed by overturning the tables. So the triumphal entry did not happen and two Gospels have the turning of the tables on that day and two have it on different days; in fact John who I quoted at the beginning:

'...scattering the coins of the money changers and overturned their tables.' (John 2:15)

You see this is chapter 2, right at the beginning of Jesus' ministry, just after he turns water into wine. (In fact, later I will show this is the most likely position) So the question we will have to answer is, why has this triumphal entry been invented?

While the Gospels may not agree on these details, the one thing they do agree on is that Jesus left Jerusalem and went to stay in Bethany that night.

'He went out to Bethany with the Twelve. (Mark 11:12)

And Matthew:

'And he left them and went out of the city to Bethany, where he spent the night.' (Mat 21:17)

And every night that week he stays at Bethany and re-enters Jerusalem five more times with no particular fuss. As Bethany appears to be a base for Jesus you need to know its location. It is identified with the present day town of al-Eizariya, located about 1.5 miles East of Jerusalem. I cannot actually tell you how long the journey takes because when I tried to walk it, I suddenly came to a huge wall right across the road that the Israelis have built. Those Wise Men trying to follow the star from Jerusalem to Bethlehem would now find the journey impossible.

There is a very revealing contradiction in the Gospels about the beginning of this day, as to how Jesus got the donkey in the first place. Luke and the other synoptic Gospels agree that Jesus cures a blind man in Jericho. Then the next verse begins:

'As he approached Bethphage and Bethany at the hill called the Mount of Olives, he sent two of his disciples, saying to them, "Go to the village ahead of you, and as you enter it you will find a colt tied there, which no one has ever ridden. Untie it and bring it here.' (Luke 19:29)

Josephus writes that the first-century road from Jericho to Jerusalem was approximately eighteen miles long. Jericho is, extraordinarily, 800 feet below sea level. A traveler walks up hill to Jerusalem, which is a tiring, 2,500 feet above sea level: an overall rise of 3,300 feet. The synoptic Gospels make it sound like Jesus travels from Jericho to Jerusalem in one day and that they just happen to pass by Bethany.

'As they approached Jerusalem and came to Bethphage and Bethany at the Mount of Olives Jesus sent two of his disciples, saying to them, "Go to the village ahead of you, and just as you enter it, you will find a colt tied there, which no one has ever ridden. Untie it and bring it here. If anyone asks you, 'Why are you doing this?' say, ' The Lord needs it and will send it back here shortly.'" (Mark 11:1)

So we have the finding of the donkey as a sort of miraculous event.

'They went and found a colt in the street, tied at a doorway. As they untied it, some people standing there asked, "What are you doing, untying that colt?" They answered as Jesus had told them to, and the people let them go.' (Mark 11:4)

Luke and Matthew have exactly the same journey, and the same miraculous discovery of the donkey.

But can you believe that Jesus walked eighteen miles from Jericho to Jerusalem, all uphill, and on the way past the house where his friends live and where he will spend every other night that week, he did not stop even to tell them that he will be back that night? He just passes by and magically picks up a donkey. And furthermore, who are these friends who live in Bethany? The occupants of the house in Bethany are never named in the synoptic Gospels yet they are clearly important people who make their house available as a base for Jesus.

So this was the Bible story till John was added to the New Testament, and then suddenly we get the names in the very first reference to Bethany in John 11:1.

'Now a man named Lazarus was sick. He was from Bethany, the village of Mary and her sister Martha."

And this is followed by a clear indication of Jesus close relationship to this family.

Now Jesus loved Martha and her sister and Lazarus."
(John 11:5)

And would you believe that after Jesus stays the night in Bethany, the next morning, lo and behold, he gets on a donkey and rides into Jerusalem!

'Jesus found a young donkey and sat on it.' (John 12:14)

So we have, as I suspected, Jesus not traveling from Jericho to Jerusalem and happening to pass by Bethany where he magically picks up a donkey, but instead we have him staying the night in Bethany and next morning:

'Jesus found a young donkey and sat on it.' (John 12:14)

So no magical instructions at all and one must ask, which is the most likely version? And remember, prior to John's Gospel being added, Lazarus, Martha and Mary were not mentioned, as living in Bethany and so the magical donkey version would appear more believable. Now it is obvious who owns the donkey. Perhaps this explains why there was reluctance by some to include John's Gospel, as he seems to deflate the whole donkey story and bring it down to earth.

Surely you must agree with me that John's version is the truth; Jesus stopped the night in Bethany and in the morning he got on the donkey and rode into Jerusalem. Originally the miraculous donkey-getting would appear to be a fact, but with the addition of John the miraculous story begins to look a bit silly as it is obvious that the donkey belongs to his beloved friends in Bethany.

You may wonder why I have gone into such detail over this one day? The reason is because we are trying to unravel the secret known by esoteric groups, and one of these groups was the Knights Templar. When the rules of the Templars were created at the council of Troyes in 1129 the most curious of oaths was imposed on all new Templar Knights:

'Obedience to Bethany, the castle of Mary and Martha'

So is there something more to Bethany and the people who live there that seems to have caused the early church a problem that they are not named in the original Bible story?

Is this the beginning of an attempt to sideline Mary Magdalene? Only when John was added were the names of the occupants of Bethany revealed to us.

Unfortunately this Templar oath has been ignored by researchers as if it were just an odd curiosity that had no real bearing on Templar beliefs. But why not an oath of allegiance to the Pope, or the Church, or to Jesus himself?

In 1307 the Templars were attacked as heretics but what was the heresy that these devout Christian Knights believed? Could it have anything to do with their seemingly inoffensive oath of obedience to the dwelling in Bethany occupied by Mary and Martha? The incredible answer is yes! And their extraordinary details will unfold over the following pages of this book, which without doubt, contains what Poussin suggested, *"Nobody else will ever rediscover in the centuries to come.'*

Chapter Two

THE MYSTERY OF BETHANY

'Obedience to Bethany, the castle of Mary and Martha'

If the vanquished, Templars swore an initiation oath of allegiance to the obscure inhabitants of Bethany and their castle, it cannot have been an unimportant curiosity to be ignored, as it has been over the years. It must have been important, so let us look at the events that are said to take place in Bethany. We have of course already mentioned that Jesus seemed to use this house, or castle as a base and another event that appears to occur there is the anointing.

Let us start by making it clear, who, when, where and even how this anointing took place. You may think it is quite obvious:

'Six days before the Passover, Jesus came to Bethany, where Lazarus lived, whom Jesus had raised from the dead. Here a dinner was given in Jesus' honor. Martha served, while Lazarus was among those reclining at the table with him. Then Mary took about a pint of pure nard, an expensive perfume; she poured it on Jesus' feet and wiped his feet with her hair.' (John 12:1)

So according to John, this event is happening in Bethany, and it is Mary, one of the women of the house who is doing the anointing and it is on the feet. That appears to be pretty conclusive, that is until you read Luke's Gospel:

'Jesus went to the Pharisee's house and reclined at the table. A woman in that town who lived a sinful life learned

that Jesus was eating at the Pharisee's house, so she came there with an alabaster jar of perfume. As she stood behind him at his feet weeping, she began to wet his feet with her tears. Then she wiped them with her hair, kissed them and poured perfume on them. When the Pharisee who had invited him saw this, he said to himself, "If this man were a prophet, he would know who is touching him and what kind of woman she is—that she is a sinner." (Luke 7:36)

Well that throws a spanner in the works, the only thing these two Gospels agree on is the expensive perfume being poured on the feet and wiped with the hair. On all the other points we are left with just one choice, which witness do we actually believe, John or Luke? Surely the woman anointing Jesus is not a sinner from the city, she is, Mary, the woman of the house as is stated again in John when introducing the raising of Lazarus.

'Now a certain man was sick, Lazarus of Bethany, the village of Mary and her sister, Martha. It was the Mary who anointed the Lord with ointment, and wiped His feet with her hair, whose brother Lazarus was sick.' (John 11.1)

Why has Luke suggested it is not Mary but a sinner from the city? What city? Jerusalem? Has this sinner traveled all the way from Jerusalem to Bethany to anoint Jesus feet? And who let her in the house since the supposed owner of the house in Luke, the Pharisee, clearly does not like her since he thinks:

"'If this man were a prophet, he would know who is touching him and what kind of woman she is—that she is a sinner."

Luke admits he never knew Jesus and has no original material about him, but chooses to contradict all the other three witnesses which are supposed to be the source of his knowledge.

GOSPEL	WHO	PLACE	HOUSE OF
John	Mary	Bethany	Lazarus + sisters
Mark	Woman	Bethany	Simon the Leper
Matthew	Woman	Bethany	Simon the Leper
Luke	Sinner	?	A Pharisee

So where did Luke get this information about a sinner from the city? Did he read it in a source that we have no knowledge of, or did he just invent it? If so why blacken the character of the anointer? And what is his problem with Bethany that he seems unable to name the place when all the others agree it is the village where the anointing took place. Can we also agree that, if this is Bethany then it is the house of Lazarus and his sisters? So who is the leper called Simon? Surely if he is a leper why would anyone go to dinner there? And would he be wealthy enough to play host to Jesus and his full entourage. Or is it a person called Simon who was once a leper and has since been healed but cannot get rid of the unfortunate moniker. Perhaps Lazarus is his second name, Simon Lazarus. Or could it be Lazarus' father and the kids are teasing their dad for some reason by calling him a leper? I cannot say that any of these possibilities sound feasible.

There is one obvious possible explanation, John is correct and the text of Mark and Matthew has been doctored to remove the owner of the house's name, which is Lazarus. You obviously cannot see any reason why Lazarus' name should be removed and replaced by Simon the Leper. But you may be shocked to find out that not only has Lazarus name been removed as owner of the house, but

Lazarus himself is totally absent from the synoptic Gospels. Yes you heard that right. It seems hard to imagine that this important person has slipped by especially as John's Gospel was a late addition. So originally, the brother of Mary and Martha was not in the Bible at all, which is why he is not named as the owner of the house. Instead a leper called Simon replaces him. I will show later, the evidence that he was actually cut out of the Synoptic Gospels. And the question is, why? Why was the brother of Mary and Martha cut from the synoptic Gospels? Does it relate to the character assassination of the Magdalene?

As all three Synoptic Gospels have removed all trace of this important, young, rich follower of Jesus, this certainly makes Lazarus, what we would call, 'a leper' when it comes to the original Bible. What is described as the very first Christian Bible 'The Evagelicon' written in 144 AD by Marcon of Sinope, not only does not mention Lazarus but also does not even mention Bethany.

If you are still not convinced that Lazarus was cut from the synoptics, look at this from Luke:

'Jesus went to the Pharisee's house and reclined at the table...'

Now Mark:

'While Jesus was in Bethany, reclining at the table...'

So we have Jesus reclining at the table but then add the Gospel of John and we find:

'Martha served, while Lazarus was among those reclining at the table with Him.'

So we see the word recline used in all four, but in the three synoptics the person Jesus is reclining with, has disappeared! Surely we are either looking at collusion between the witnesses to remove Lazarus or one of the synoptic writers has doctored the other two. It is already becoming obvious who the culprit is, but what is missing is any motive. And it is this motive that throws light on the odd oath of allegiance taken by the Knights Templar.

For now let us try to establish who did the anointing, and if you think the owner of the house was a problem wait till you try to establish the woman doing the anointing, it is a veritable minefield.

You have seen the actual wording of John who says it is Mary, while Luke says it is a sinner from the city; so we better take a look at Mark:

'While he was in Bethany, reclining at the table in the home of Simon the Leper, a woman came with an alabaster jar of very expensive perfume, made of pure nard. (Mark 14:3)

Remember Matthew's version is almost word for word the same as Mark, just calling her *'a woman'*.

As they don't name this woman they don't actually contradict John, so her name could be Mary. It is only Luke who actually contradicts John since he clearly states she is not the woman of the house but from the city, and a sinner to boot.

Okay you could disagree with Luke and say you believe John, and this is Mary the sister of Lazarus. But the confusion does not end there because the church has entered the fray with several pronouncements.

When Jacapo di Voragine the 13th century Archbishop of Genoa, wrote up the *'Life of Mary Magdalene'*, from church records, he stated that

'Mary possessed the heritage of the castle of Bethany'.

So this Mary was actually Mary Magdalene, and for centuries she it was who anointed Jesus with her hair. But then suddenly the church invented a new Mary called, Mary of Bethany, who was the anointer. So now there are three: a sinner, Mary of Bethany or Mary Magdalene. Not only that but this invented Mary of Bethany was made a Saint and there are churches actually dedicated to her, while poor Mary Magdalene was reduced to being a prostitute and had to wait till modern times to become a saint. What is the Church's problem with Mary Magdalene there is no evidence that she was a prostitute and why invent another person to do the anointing? Was it to remove the importance of Mary Magdalene?

We know all portrayals of Mary Magdalene whether saint or harlot, have the alabaster jar. The age-old convention when painting the Magdalene was to give her red hair, a green or red dress but always with the alabaster jar to anoint Jesus in Bethany.

It is of no use suggesting the painters got it wrong, this has nothing to do with the painters; they didn't come up with these conventions; it was the church who commissioned the work and you can bet your bottom dollar if the painter had left out the alabaster jar, the commissioning church would have sent the painting straight back.

Mary Magdalene and the anointing pose such a problem for the church that, whatever doctrinal strategies are imposed to downgrade her position they all self-destruct. With the church fluctuating on this, you can sometimes be a heretic *(a person who differs in opinion from established religious dogma)* for believing the Magdalene did the anointing, while other times you were fine. I am afraid this whole affair rather plays into the hands of those who think the Gospel story is just a total invention.

Is the Church embarrassed about something to do with the relationship between Magdalene and Jesus? Certainly there are those who consider Jesus and Mary were married. I am not so sure for a number of reasons that will come up later, but if you want confirmation that Mary Magdalene anoints Jesus feet and is the sister of Martha and Lazarus, you need look no further than churches dedicated to the Magdalene. Take, for instance, the beautiful, Gaudi inspired church of Santuario Santa Magdalena, in Alicante, very worth a visit for the architecture.

As you approach the church, there she is, the Magdalene, wiping Jesus' feet with her hair.

And inside are paintings of the Magdalene at the raising of Lazarus, Magdalene sitting with Jesus as Martha does the preparation and Magdalene anointing the feet. I should mention one other painting that you will always find in Magdalene churches; it is the Magdalene in a cave with a skull.

This is not a representation of anything in the Gospels but is of great significance and we will consider the implication of this painting later.

So what is wrong with Mary Magdalene that she has to be, either blackened, or cut out of almost all the Gospels?

'And the twelve were with him, Mary called Magdalene, out of whom had come seven demons, and Joanna the wife of Chuza,

Herod's steward, and many others who provided for him from their substance.' (Luke 8)

Out of whom seven demons had come – if it is true it is an exorcism, but this statement is used by the church to make the Magdalene a prostitute. In fact one Pope decided that the seven demons were actually the seven deadly sins, pride, envy, gluttony, greed, lust, sloth, and wrath and heaped all these on top of prostitution. So the Magdalene was a fat, greedy, lazy, jealous, angry prostitute! They don't pull their punches when it comes to slandering Mary Magdalene, do they?

Who started all this? If you take a look at the end of Mark's Gospel, just after the body of Jesus is missing from the tomb (16:8) you will find in most modern Bibles this odd statement before 16:9:

['The most reliable early manuscripts and other ancient witnesses do not have Mark 16:9–to–20']

To put it bluntly, Mark 16:9–20 is an accepted forgery! Mark had the body missing but, extraordinarily, he never had Jesus resurrecting! Now look at what starts this fake addition.

'After He had risen early on the first day of the week, He first appeared to Mary Magdalene, from whom He had cast out seven demons.' (Mark 16:9)

As Mark's Gospel has no such defamatory description of Mary Magdalene and the seven demons, this supposed clarification would actually be totally confusing to an early reader because Mark never wrote anything about these seven demons in the text. We know this description comes from Luke's Gospel that had not yet been written! When Luke took Mark's Gospel and wrote his version, he also seems to have tampered with Mark, adding the resurrection with his own very specific description of Mary Magdalene. And did he also doctor Mark and Matthew to extract Lazarus? And was he the person who removed the night at Bethany when in the morning they get the donkey? All three synoptics have exactly the same strange wording, adding Bethphage before Bethany.

'As they approached Jerusalem and came to Bethphage and Bethany at the Mount of Olives'.

Which village are they coming to, Bethphage or Bethany? I must admit I think this is Luke's handiwork, demoting Bethany by placing another village ahead of it. But if it is not Luke then it is someone who has his same agenda against those living in Bethany, whom the Templars swore allegiance to. Are we witnessing a major disagreement between Luke and the Templars, who are actually a thousand years apart! As Luke is very much the author who most represents the Roman Church's story of Jesus, then can we say the Templar oath is actually a slap in the face to the church of Rome.

I am no expert on language and style, but those who are, say Luke wrote Acts of the Apostles, which basically ignores the acts of the Apostles and is actually mainly the story of Paul, with a bit about Peter, but what about those in Bethany? *'Now Jesus loved Martha and her sister and Lazarus.'* These people who are so loved by Jesus, where are they in Acts of the Apostles? Like Thomas and most of the other Disciples they disappear.

Who then is this Luke who has a problem with Bethany?

'Demas, having loved this present world, has deserted me and gone to Thessalonica; Crescens has gone to Galatia, Titas to Dalmatia. Only Luke is with me. (2 Timothy 4:10)

This same Luke is mentioned again in Philemon 1:24, as *'my fellow worker.'* So this is our writer who presumably followed Paul to Rome. I should also add that reading one academic paper I found this:

'The Pauline character of the Luke Gospel has been frequently commented on. It is curious to observe how much more this is pronounced in the first edition.'

This seems to confirms my belief that this is Paul's traveling companion who is doing a re-write to present his version of Mark's Gospel, but with certain clear prejudices. Are these prejudices Paul's or did they develop in Luke after Paul's death? Of course it is Paul who is named with Peter as the founder of the Christian Church of Rome, so are they responsible for the Church's attitude to Bethany and the inhabitants? If so, why?

Now before we leave the anointing we have to confront one other aspect where the Gospels disagree. What part of Jesus body was anointed? The fuller description suggests the feet and I have yet to find a Magdalene Church that has her anointing the head, it is usually the feet. So why do two Gospels switch it to the head? There are two possible reasons; firstly I did get my girlfriend to wipe my feet with her hair (all in the name of research, I assure you) and it did actually seem a very sexual act. So perhaps it was switched for that reason.

But my favored idea is that Jesus was presented as the Jewish Messiah, a word that actually means the *'anointed one'* so there had to be an anointment. The question then is, who anointed him? And the only answer in the Bible is this event in Bethany. But the anointing has to be on the head not the feet, so I suspect that was the thinking behind the switching to the head by two of the Gospels. Furthermore the title, Christ is also meant to translate as *'the anointed,'* so without an anointment he cannot be Jesus Christ. And so they appear to have placed such an anointment at a meal to replicate Psalm 23: *'Thou preparest a table before me in the presence of mine enemies: thou anointest my head with oil; my cup runneth over.'*

So the switch to the head appears to be to fulfill the Psalm and anoint Jesus as the Messiah, the Christ. But actually Mary cannot anoint someone to make them the Messiah; it has to be a priest and usually a special Zadok priest. My mum could not have anointed Prince Charles to make him King; it has to be the Archbishop as it is the moment of dedication to God and the country. I hope you have noticed that this event, whether feet or head, is always called *'the anointing of Jesus'* but nobody adding perfume to their feet would say, I have anointed myself, other than as a joke.

The *'Anointing'* like the *'Triumphal Entry'* are two headline description of events that did not happen. Here is a typical example from my Bible:

Jesus Anointed at Bethany

14 Now the Passover and the Festival of Unleavened Bread were only two days away,

If I am right then it does suggest they were desperate to get Jesus anointed and there was actually no other moment they could find that suggested this process took place. But had they not mentioned any anointing then one could say he was anointed but it was not reported and no one would be much the wiser. But moving the perfume from the feet to the head – can I say – smells distinctly fishy.

The mysterious little church of Rennes-le-Château dedicated to the Magdalene, always has interesting heretical details that help us. There are hundreds of books about how the Priest, Abbé Saunière suddenly became rich and with this inexplicable money carried out major works on the church. And vital to us is that he inserted heretical information in many of the stained-glass windows and statues he erected. Behind the altar is the main stained glass window of the church.

It depicts Mary Magdalene with her alabaster jar wiping the feet of Jesus with her hair, and significantly her brother Lazarus reclining next to him. Furthermore, to the left of the altar is another window which tells the story where Jesus rebukes Martha:

"Lord, don't you care that my sister has left me to do all the preparations? Tell her to help me!"' (Luke 10:38)

Clearly in this church, Martha is the sister of Mary Magdalene and therefore her brother is Lazarus. And if you want further confirmation, the priest, Sauniére built a house next to the Church called Villa Bethanie and next to it a library called Magdala, which in Aramaic means tower and is thought to be the origin of the name Magdalene

But look at it, with its castle crenellations. Was the original Bethany building a castle? The tower looks to me like the castle on a chessboard. Did I read somewhere that the Templars brought back the game of chess after learning it from the Saracens.

KNIGHTS TEMPLAR PLAYING CHESS 1283

It certainly arrived in Europe from that area and strangely the church have banned chess at different times over the centuries. One thing to remember is that the checkerboard floor is an integral part of the Freemason's lodge, and a lot of ceremonial moves are made around the squares.

While we are mentioning games, it should be noted that playing cards were also introduced by the Knights Templar. The original picture cards carry heretical stories, which is why they were also banned by the church. The twenty two picture cards of the major arcana no longer exist in our present playing cards, having all been banned, except the uninitiated *'Fool'* card which became the joker in the pack. But study the images and you will find many interesting details, like the *Hanged Man* has crossed leg similar to Templar grave carvings. On the square.

And the *High Priestess* sits between the Templar pillars of Boaz and Jachin and holds the Jewish Holy book, 'The Torah'. Could this be Mary Magdalene? One thing that most people forget about the Magdalene is that she was born a Jew and died a Jew, Christianity had not yet separated from Judaism, not till after Paul got to Rome in 62 AD

I should report, hot off the press, the latest Vatican News:

"Pope Francis elevated the memory of Mary Magdalene to the status of Festivity on July 22nd, 2016 in order to stress the importance of this faithful disciple of Christ." (Vatican News)

About time too.

That completes our investigation of the anointing and what we have discovered is that accepting the importance of the Bethany family does seem to put you in opposition to Luke. But can this inoffensive belief be a factor in making you a heretic and placing you in the front line for burning at the stake? That does seem a little bit extreme.

Chapter Three

THE RAISING OF LAZARUS

Lazarus is clearly an important character in the Jesus story and the act of resurrecting him from the dead is said to attract attention.

'A large crowd of Jews found out that Jesus was there and came, not only because of him but also to see Lazarus, whom he had raised from the dead. So the chief priests made plans to kill Lazarus as well.' (John12: 9)

Did I say important, I should have said Lazarus is extremely important, in fact vital to the Jesus story as they are both threatened with death at the hands of the Chief Priests. So why then, if he was that important, does he not appear in any of the synoptic Gospels? Is there something he did that upset those who established the Church of Rome? Or is there something damning in the raising of Lazarus story? If so why was it allowed into the Bible in John's Gospel? Certainly John's Gospel was added later, and although there were those who did not want it included, it does seem to have passed the censors, or perhaps the original censors were dead and the new censors considered it safe by then. It certainly has appeared safe, as nobody has raised any damning information from John's Gospel as yet. But it is not safe; it is not safe at all, but very revealing and absolutely damning.

'Now a man named Lazarus was sick. He was from Bethany, the village of Mary and her sister Martha. [This Mary, was the

same one who poured perfume on the Lord and wiped his feet with her hair. So the sisters sent word to Jesus, "Lord, the one you love is sick". (John 11:2)
Then Jesus said to them plainly, Lazarus is dead. (John 11:14)
Now Jesus loved Martha and her sister and Lazarus.
(Note: Not sure why they removed Mary's name)

So when he heard that Lazarus was sick, he stayed where he was two more days, and then he said to his disciples, "Let us go back to Judea."
"But Rabbi," they said, "a short while ago the Jews there tried to stone you, and yet you are going back?"
(Note: This contradicts a later statement in John that, the Romans do not allow the Jews to stone people.)

"Our friend Lazarus has fallen asleep; but I am going there to wake him up."
His disciples replied, "Lord, if he sleeps, he will get better."
Jesus had been speaking of his death, but his disciples thought he meant natural sleep.
So then he told them plainly, "Lazarus is dead, and for your sake I am glad I was not there, so that you may believe. But let us go to him."
Then Thomas (also known as Didymus) said to the rest of the disciples, "Let us also go, that we may die with him."
(Note: Ask yourself why they would want to die with him?)

On his arrival, Jesus found that Lazarus had already been in the tomb for four days. Now Bethany was less than two miles from Jerusalem, and many Jews had come to Martha and Mary to comfort them in the loss of their brother. When Martha heard that Jesus was coming, she went out to meet him, but Mary stayed at home.

"Lord," Martha said to Jesus, "if you had been here, my brother would not have died. But I know that even now God will give you whatever you ask."

Jesus said to her, "Your brother will rise again."

Martha answered, "I know he will rise again in the resurrection at the last day."

After she had said this, she went back and called her sister Mary. "The Rabbi is here, and is asking for you." When Mary heard this, she got up quickly and went to him.

(Note: Some people who believe Jesus was married suggest that if Mary is sitting shiva in the house, as a wife she is not allowed to leave until instructed by her husband, according to Jewish custom.)

When Mary reached the place where Jesus was and saw him, she fell at his feet and said, "Lord, if you had been here, my brother would not have died." When Jesus saw her weeping, and the Jews who had come along with her also weeping, he was deeply moved in spirit and troubled. "Where have you laid him?" he asked.

"Come and see, Lord," they replied.

Jesus wept.

Then the Jews said, "See how he loved him!"

But some of them said, "Could not he who opened the eyes of the blind man have kept this man from dying?"

Jesus, once more deeply moved, came to the tomb. It was a cave with a stone laid across the entrance. "Take away the stone," he said.

"But, Lord," said Martha, the sister of the dead man, "by this time there is a bad odor, for he has been there four days."

Then Jesus said, "Did I not tell you that if you believe, you will see the glory of God?"

So they took away the stone. Then Jesus looked up and said, "Father, I thank you that you have heard me. I knew that you always hear me, but I said this for the benefit of the people standing here, that they may believe that you sent me."

When he had said this, Jesus called in a loud voice, "Lazarus, come out!" The dead man came out, his hands and feet wrapped with strips of linen, and a cloth around his face. Jesus said to them, "Take off the grave clothes and let him go."

Let us go back to a key statement at the beginning. When Jesus tells them Lazarus is dead, Thomas says, *"Let us also go, that we may die with him."* What can Thomas possibly mean by that? Do they all want to go and catch his disease and die too? Or are they thinking to go there and commit suicide and die with their comrade? Surely not! I can give you one possible answer and it comes from the rituals of the Freemasons. In third degree initiation the Lodge is darkened and the novitiate, who is about to be made a Master Mason, is laid to death on a shroud with a skull and crossed bones over his head. Here is an image of the process.

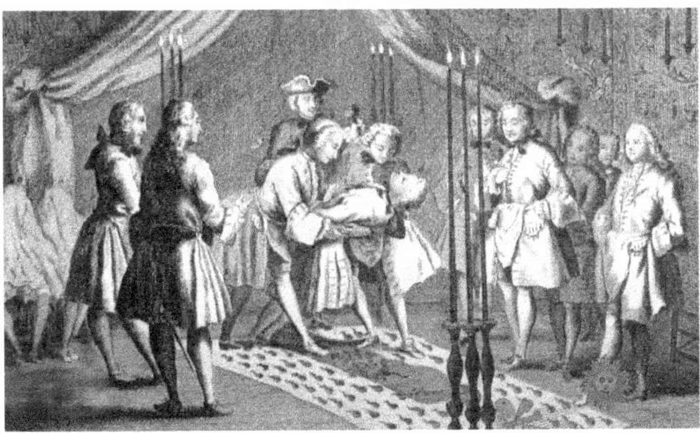

Then the Master offers the secret grip, and the novitiate is hinged up from the grave by the Masters, whispering the magic words, as they resurrect him back to life as a Master Mason. A death and rebirth ritual. That would certainly make sense as to why the others would want to die and be resurrected into the next stage of initiation. It would also explain Jesus delay in returning.

'So when he heard that Lazarus was sick, he stayed where he was two more days, and then he said to his disciples, "Let us go back to Judea." (John 11:6)

It is usual in these rituals to stay in Hades for three days, and Jesus' delay till the third day reinforces the idea that this is a death and resurrection ritual. Here is a symbolic representation of a Masonic resurrection from the grave, using the Lion's paw grip, and taking place in Ancient Egypt, suggesting the ancient origins of the ritual.

I cant say I believe the Masonic ritual goes back that far but there certainly were death and resurrection rituals in ancient times.

Just for you information here is the Lion's paw, Master Mason grip.

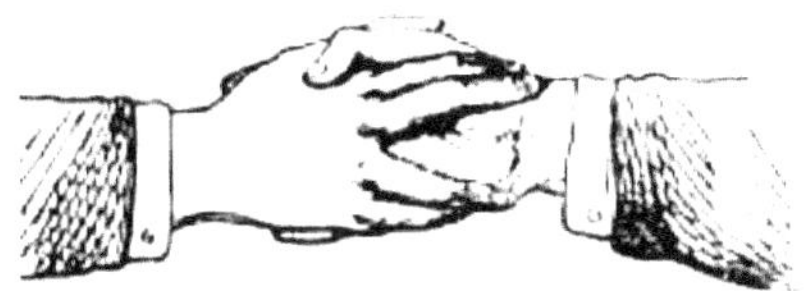

So does this explain the disciples statement *"Let us also go, that we may die with him?"* Have we any evidence that might suggest this is what is happening? A powerful Christian movement, which was sidelined by Rome, were the Gnostics. Texts relating to Gnostic beliefs were uncovered in 1945 in Egypt and in one work, *The Treatise on Resurrection,* it states that human existence is spiritual death and the resurrection is the moment of enlightenment. Whoever grasps this idea becomes spiritually alive and can be resurrected from the dead immediately.

Another Gnostic document, the *Gospel of Philip* ridicules 'ignorant Christians who take the resurrection literally':

'Those who say they will die first and then rise are in error, they must receive the resurrection while they live."

What evidence have we that there were levels of initiation in early Christianity? Well there is a letter from Clement of Alexandria written around 180 AD.

"When Peter was martyred, Mark went to Alexandria, bringing both his knowledge and the things he remembered hearing from Peter. He arranged a more spiritual gospel for the use of those being perfected. Nevertheless, he did not reveal the things, which are not to be discussed. He did not write out the hierophantic instruction of the Lord, but added other deeds to the ones he had already written. Then, he added certain sayings, the interpretation of which he knew

would initiate the hearers into the innermost sanctuary of the truth, which has been hidden seven times. And when he died, he left his writing to the church in Alexandria, where it is even now still extremely carefully guarded, being read only to those who have been initiated into the greatest mysteries."

This states that Jesus is a hierophant, which is somebody who initiates others into occult mysteries? It also states that Mark wrote a second more spiritual Gospel for those being Perfected, that unfortunately we have never seen or heard of. But who is this Mark who Peter trusted with this secret knowledge? We have no way of knowing for certain but let me speculate.

 'When Jesus came into Peter's home, He saw his mother-in-law lying sick in bed with a fever. He touched her hand, and the fever left her; and she got up and served Him.'(Mat. 8:14)

If Peter had a Mother in Law he had to have a wife! Because it is a bit obscure it seems to have escaped any editing. But in fact Paul actually complains in a letter that many of the disciples have wives. So Peter has a wife and so one imagines he has children. Just look at this at the end of one of Peter's letters.

"She who is in Babylon, chosen together with you, sends you her greetings, and so does my son Mark." 1 Peter 5:13

So this strongly suggests that Mark is Peter's son who writes the Gospel of Mark. He is not a witness himself but he is simply reporting the stories of Peter. This is confirmed by Papias who was quoted by Eusebius.

'Mark, who had indeed been Peter's interpreter, wrote down accurately but not in order as much as he remembered about what was either said or done by the Lord. For he neither

heard the Lord nor followed him, but later, as I said, Peter, who would give his teachings as needed, but not, as it were, making a compilation of the dominical oracles, so that Mark did not fail at all by writing some of them as he recalled. For he took care of one thing, to omit nothing of what he heard or falsify anything among them. (Church History 3.39.14-16)

Clearly this does not confirm without question that Peter's son, Mark wrote the Gospel but he is certainly a prime candidate, especially as Peter passed on some very confidential information about levels of initiation to Mark, so one assumes an intimacy, or at least a level of trust between the two existed.

The letter I quoted, written by the second century Christian father, Clement of Alexandria, has an interesting history. In 1958 Morton Smith, a professor of ancient history, found this letter in the Monastery of Mar Saba with reference to a missing piece of Mark. Luckily he photographed the letters in black and white and four scholars who visited in 1976 photographed it in color. I say luckily because subsequent attempts by scholars to view the manuscripts have been unsuccessful. The letter has disappeared. Perhaps the reason is that the hidden letter mentions two sections of Mark's Gospel that had been cut. One very large section that Clement states was between verses 34 and 35 of Mark 10 is...you guessed it...none other than the story of the raising of Lazarus! We were surprised that this important story was only in John, but, lo and behold, it was in one of the synoptic Gospel, but was cut out. It begins with a very recognizable trait that probably reveals the mystery editor.

'And they come into Bethany. And a certain woman whose brother had died was there.

I am sure Mark would not have been so coy with the names, but we do recognize this trait as being Luke's handiwork, or at least someone with the same problem, with the names of those in Bethany. So this clearly has been edited first to remove the names of Lazarus and his sister, Mary, but then they decided they just could not stomach any of it, so the whole lot was cut out. (Researchers found some sections of the New Testament had been edited up to six times.)

But let us continue with Mark's hidden version of the Lazarus story:

And, coming, she prostrated herself before Jesus and says to him "Son of David, have mercy on me." But the disciples rebuked her. And Jesus, being angered, went off with her into the garden where the tomb was, and straightaway a great cry was heard from the tomb. And going near Jesus rolled away the stone from the door of the tomb. And straightaway, going in where the youth was, he stretched forth his hand and raised him, seizing his hand. But the youth, looking upon him, loved him and began to beseech him that he might be with him. And going out of the tomb they came into the house of the youth, for he was rich. And after six days Jesus told him what to do and in the evening the youth comes to him, wearing a linen cloth over his naked body. And he remained with him that night, for Jesus taught him the mystery of the kingdom of God. And thence, arising, he returned to the other side of the Jordan.' (Secret Mark)

Firstly what is clear is that the tomb is in the garden of the house in Bethany. This is not London where every house has a little garden. Gardens in the Middle East are usually in Palaces or at least very large houses or possibly castles?

'And straightway a great cry was heard from the tomb.'

Is Lazarus dead, if so how can he cry out even before the stone is rolled away? What follows does seem to reinforce the theory, that this is a death and resurrection ritual:

'And straightaway, going in where the youth was, Jesus stretched forth his hand and raised him, seizing his hand.

The emphasis on, *seizing his hand,* even sounds like the magic grip used to raise the novitiate in Freemasonry.

But the youth, looking upon him, loved him and began to beseech him that he might be with him. And going out of the tomb they came into the house of the youth, for he was rich. And after six days Jesus told him what to do.' (Secret Mark)

That seems to confirm that Jesus is a Hierophant initiating the novice into secret knowledge.

'... and in the evening the youth comes to him, wearing a linen cloth over his naked body. And he remained with him that night, for Jesus taught him the mystery of the kingdom of God.'

I am having real trouble thinking of an innocent interpretation of this event between Jesus and Lazarus. I know Gays like to quote this episode. What do you make of it? Does this suggest that Lazarus is the 'disciple Jesus loved' literally? Perhaps you could argue that this seemingly lurid association was never in the Gospel, but luckily the youth appears later in our present day Mark, using the same Greek word *'neaniskos'* for him, reinforcing the fact that this Lazarus story was once in Mark. This is from the arrest of Jesus?

'A young man, wearing nothing but a linen garment, was following Jesus. When they seized him, he fled naked, leaving his garment behind.' (Mark 14:51)

I think we can be safe to say this raising of Lazarus was in Mark's Gospel, but first the names were edited out (which does suggest Luke's handiwork) and then the whole event was removed at a very early date because we have no version of Mark with it in. When John's Gospel was incorporated into the Bible the problem with Bethany seems to have been solved (or perhaps Luke is dead now) and the Church felt able to mention Lazarus.

The Magdalene window in Notre Dame d'Chartes Cathedral has all the events in the Magdalene's story including those that may have been denied by the Church at the time. Here is the central one of three that tell the Lazarus story.

I should add that you have read several times about the young man in a linen cloth over his naked body, which does suggest a ritual is taking place. This is because you will find linen is always used in ceremonies.

Even in Masonic initiation where the novitiate is hoodwinked and slipshod with a noose round his neck, he wears a linen suit over his naked body (actually nowadays they keep their underpants on.) Leather and wool come from dead animals and are therefore unclean in the complex classification of clean and unclean in Jewish law, so linen is used in ceremonies.

Perhaps the letter from Clement can give us another clue, because he admits to another cut in Mark's Gospel. If you read Mark 10:46 there is clearly something missing:

'Then they came to Jericho. As Jesus and his disciples, together with a large crowd, were leaving the city.'

They go to Jericho – they leave Jericho, so what happened in Jericho? Well, I can't tell you much, as it was, like the names in Bethany, edited out in a first cut, but here is the remainder in Clements' own words:

'After the words, "And they came to Jericho," the secret Gospel adds only, "And the sister of the youth whom Jesus loved and his mother and Salome were there, and Jesus did not receive them".

Adds only!! Is he joking? Somebody cut the text to leave this nonsense, where Jesus arrives in Jericho, these people are there, but he didn't see them! Ridiculous. I would love to see what was cut here because if Clement can't even repeat it, it must have been something very revealing.

Actually the little bit that Clement gave out about Jericho does tell us something. In John's Gospel there is an un-named disciple called *'the disciple Jesus loved'* and there has been much speculation as to who it is. So this is an interesting piece of information, that the un-named, beloved disciple has a sister:

'And the sister of the youth whom Jesus loved and his mother and Salome were there,'

So this tells us that the beloved disciple had a sister. Also this definitely looks like the names were again removed from this before the whole section was removed. If Clement can't even reveal what happened in Jericho, it could well be an event between Jesus and the un-named *sister of the* un-named *youth Jesus loved*. Who is this guy who keeps removing names from the Gospels? I know who I think it is.

Chapter Four

THE DISCIPLE JESUS LOVED

Let us look objectively at the references to the beloved disciple, which now only appears in John's Gospel but, according to Clements letter, was once in Mark. In Dan Brown's famous book, 'The Da Vinci Code' he takes a look at Leonardo's painting of the Last Supper and declares that sitting on Jesus right is the Beloved Disciple and it looks like a woman. So from this he concludes that Leonardo is secretly suggesting that this is the Magdalene and Leonardo has sacrilegiously put her in the Last Supper. This idea is easily dispelled by John's statement at the Crucifixion.

'When Jesus saw his mother there, and the disciple whom he loved standing nearby, he said to her, "Woman, here is your son". (John 19:25)

And even the bit cut from Mark suggests the same:

'And the sister of the youth whom Jesus loved.'

So the beloved disciple is clearly male and has a sister. What about Dan Brown's idea that anyway it looks like a woman? I would just point out that Leonardo was probably gay (he was never married and at 24 was had up for Sodomy charges) Just look at this painting by another gay painter Caravaggio, *'The Supper at Emmaus.'*

In John Berger's 'Ways of Seeing' this painting was shown to adults who said it was Jesus, while children shown the very same painting said it was a woman! When I do film directing master classes, I show them this painting and tell the potential directors that they need to look at things with the eyes of a child. By the way I also show them Michelangelo's 'David'. If this has anything to do with the biblical character, I'll eat my hat. This is a gay guy, enjoying sculpting a gorgeous young man's body: and why not? I get the same feeling of adoration when I film beautiful young naked women.

Of course if you suggest the Magdalene is one of the people in Leonardo's 'Last Supper' that leaves only eleven disciples in the painting. And anyway it is not so sacrilegious to paint the Magdalene at the last supper; Fra Angelico painted one such Last Supper with the Magdalene present.

Let us look at the first reference to the 'beloved disciple' in the Gospels. This occurs during the Last Supper, where our young man sits next to Jesus, reclining on his bosom, fielding questions from the other disciples, suggesting a somewhat higher status.

'Jesus said, "Most assuredly, I say to you, one of you will betray me." Then the disciples looked at one another, perplexed about whom He spoke. Now there was leaning on Jesus' bosom one of His disciples, whom Jesus loved. Simon Peter therefore motioned to him to ask who it was of whom He spoke. Then, leaning back on Jesus' breast, he said to Him, "Lord, who is it?"
Jesus answered, "It is he to whom I shall give a piece of bread when I have dipped it." (John 13:22)

I have lots of fun looking at paintings trying to depict this odd situation. It is so difficult to place the beloved disciple that does not look awkward, *leaning on Jesus' bosom'.*

This painting looks like the beloved disciple has either dropped his fork or is doing something rude to Jesus.

Sometimes the beloved disciple is shown asleep, which is rather strange as he is chatting to Peter, other paintings show him as a small boy sitting on Jesus lap. I love this one where he is both a boy and asleep.

So this sleeping boy who is supposed to be chatting to Peter, is said by the Academic world to be the disciple, John. They come to this conclusion from the last lines of John's Gospel:

'Peter turned and saw that the disciple whom Jesus loved was following them. This was the one, who had leaned on his breast at the supper and had said, "Lord, who is going to betray you?"
When Peter saw him, he asked, "Lord, what about him?"
Jesus answered, "If I want him to remain alive until I return, what is that to you? You must follow me".

This has the possible meaning that Peter will die for following Jesus, but the 'beloved disciple' will remain alive. It could also suggest that Peter is already dead and the author is justifying why he himself is still alive. This is followed by the final words of John's Gospel:

'This is the disciple who testifies to these things and who wrote them down. We know that his testimony is true. Jesus

did many other things as well. If every one of them were written down, I suppose that even the whole world would not have room for the books that would be written.' (John 21:20)

Right, this is clearly saying that whoever wrote this Gospel is the 'beloved disciple'. So the answer should be John, and most Christians say John is the beloved disciple. But unfortunately the Gospel writers are unknown; names were given to the testimonies much later. I personally believe that Mark was written by someone called Mark for reasons I gave, but he was an associate of Peter in Rome and clearly not a disciple, as there is no disciple called Mark. The other difficulty is that John's Gospel appears to have three different authors. Perhaps one of them was the 'beloved disciple' and his work was added to by a person called John.

I can certainly prove the writer was not John, who was a Galilean fisherman. First take biblical expert, Professor Elaine Pagels rhetorical question:

'Could a fisherman from Galilee have written the elegant, spare, philosophically sophisticated prose of this Gospel?'

And, add to this what other commentators have said about John's Gospel – that the author knew Jerusalem well, as is evident from the geographic and place name information throughout the book. He mentions, among others, the Sheep Gate Pool (Bethesda), the Siloam Pool and Jacob's Well. So the writer knows Jerusalem well. But what about Galilee? He hasn't got a clue about the area and the fishermen there. In John's first verse we read of Jesus claiming Phillip lives in Bethsaida, *the city of Andrew and Peter*. Yet Andrew and Peter are from Capernaum not Bethsaida. (Mark. 1:21) Then in John 12:21 we are told that Philip *was of Bethsaida of Galilee*. Yet Bethsaida is not in the province of Galilee! Is then the writer of John, a Galilean fisherman, or a man from Bethany, the suburbs of Jerusalem? The same man whom Jesus is said to love?

'Now Jesus loved Martha and her sister and Lazarus.'
(John 11:5)

And later in the same story:

"Where have you laid him?" Jesus asked. "Come and see, Lord," they replied. Jesus wept. Then the Jews said, "See how he loved him!" (John 11:36)

Is it becoming obvious who the beloved disciple is? Here then is a full description of him and of his family and where they lived.

'Now a man named Lazarus was sick. He was from Bethany, the village of Mary and her sister Martha. [This Mary, was the same one who poured perfume on the Lord and wiped his feet with her hair]. So the sisters sent word to Jesus, "Lord, the one you love is sick". (John 11:2)

Let me repeat that last statement.

'The sisters sent a letter to Him saying, "Lord, behold, he whom you love is sick."

Who is sick? *'The one whom you love.'* And who could that be? No name or other clue of any sort. So tell us Jesus, in your own words, who is this sick person who you love?

Then Jesus said to them plainly, Lazarus is dead. (John 11:14)

But one of the great mysteries in Biblical research is *'who was the Disciple Jesus loved?'* And the usual answer is the disciple, John. While in Dan Brown's book 'The Da Vinci Code' he ponders on this and comes up with the answer, Mary Magdalene. Why are they guessing, surely Jesus has just told us in his own words, it is Lazarus. Case solved! If there was an attempt to conceal Lazarus' name, it has not worked very well as it is plain as day that Lazarus is the beloved disciple and therefore the original writer of John's Gospel.

It was so obvious that I looked for Academic backing for my conclusion and soon found this from Professor William Brownlee, a leading Biblical scholar and one of the foremost experts of the 'Dead Sea Scrolls:

"From internal evidence in the Fourth Gospel....the conclusion is that the beloved disciple is Lazarus of Bethany."

So while everything points to Lazarus being the 'beloved disciple' we yet have no clue why there is all these machinations around concealing his name in the synoptic Gospels and taking his name off John's Gospel. Surely if they put Lazarus name into the Synoptic Gospels and called John's Gospel, 'The Gospel of Lazarus' it would be fine. Or would it?

Before we move on, I want you to look again at the stained glass window in the mysterious church at Rennes-le-Château.

Look at Lazarus who the text says is reclining next to Jesus. That position is exactly where the paintings of the Last Supper place the 'Beloved Disciple', except that both Lazarus, in this event and the 'Beloved Disciple' at the Last Supper are not sitting, they are reclining, and actually in the Last Supper, reclining on Jesus bosom. Does this suggest that the two events are actually happening at the same time? Jesus starts the Last Supper by washing the feet of his Disciples so it appears Mary then perfumes Jesus' feet. There is certainly a degree of logic in that. But what is all this reclining anyway? We are about to destroy the logic of nearly all paintings of the 'Anointing' and the 'Last Supper'. Remember the statement:

'She stood behind him at his feet, weeping, and began to bathe his feet with her tears and to dry them with her hair. Then she continued kissing his feet and anointing them with the ointment.' (Luke 7:38)

Paintings always show Jesus sitting down with Magdalene kneeling in front of him dealing with his feet.

But it clearly says *she stood behind him*! You see what this means? There is only one way she can be standing behind him yet wipe his feet with her hair. Do away with chairs and you have the answer. They are lying down like our image of a Roman banquet. This detail suggests it was the feet being anointed not the head, as that would be from the front, which makes it clear now that this was not the anointing of a king as the two later Gospels try to suggest. This also explains how Lazarus happens to be lying on Jesus breast, which is such a mess in paintings, when seated on chairs.

I apologies to all the artists who have just had their works degraded to inaccurate.

Chapter Five

THE LAST SUPPER

There may be one other possible event in Bethany that we should add here. Could the Last Supper have taken place in the house in Bethany? John's Gospel does not say where it happened, he just announces when it happened:

'Now before the Feast of the Passover when Jesus knew his time had come…' (John 13:1)

And then he goes straight into *'During Supper…'* But the synoptic Gospels have a whole new story about where the meal is taking place.

'Then came the day of Unleavened Bread, on which the Passover lamb had to be sacrificed. So Jesus sent Peter and John, saying, "Go and prepare the Passover for us, that we may eat it." They said to him, "Where will you have us prepare it?" He said to them, "Behold, when you have entered the city, a man carrying a jar of water will meet you. Follow him into the house that he enters and tell the master of the house, 'The Teacher says to you, Where is the guest room, where I may eat the Passover with my disciples?' And he will show you a large upper room furnished; prepare it there." And they went and found it just as he had told them, and they prepared the Passover. And when the hour came, he reclined at table, and the apostles with him. (Luke 22:7)

I must admit this sounds to me exactly like the story of how they magically got the donkey for Jesus trying to suggest he did not enter Bethany, when we know very well he spent the night there. Mark is almost the same.

' His disciples said to him, "Where will you have us go and prepare for you to eat the Passover?" And he sent two of his disciples and said to them, "Go into the city, and a man carrying a jar of water will meet you. Follow him, and wherever he enters, say to the master of the house, 'The Teacher says, where is my guest room, where I may eat the Passover with my disciples?' And he will show you a large upper room etc..etc.. (Mark 14:12)

Word for word, just like the donkey story, and as unbelievable. You cannot just go to an empty room and eat the Seder (the Passover meal) it requires a lot, and I mean a lot of preparation. All Jewish households would start by removing all the 'Chometz' (any food containing yeast) the day before. So not a crumb of bread must be in the house, and the following eight days the household must remain free of 'Chometz'. Secondly any Jew would laugh at the idea in the Gospel that they parted *bread* and dipped it.  Matzos are useless to dip and parting it would just snap into pieces. They are clearly talking about ordinary bread. And then later even worse: they ate *'bread'* representing the body and drank wine representing *blood*! That would, not only be disgusting to a Jew who bleeds all his meat, but in the Seder meal glasses of wine serve a particular part in the ritual.

I am pretty sure the Last Supper, is happening in Bethany and Mary, Martha and Lazarus are present. You may think I have no real grounds to suggest such a thing, but let me reassure you because unbelievably, it is accidentally admitted in an early church document. In attempting to downgrade women and especially Mary Magdalene, the *'Apostolic Church Order'* makes a huge mistake.

'When the Master blessed the bread and the cup, and assigned them with the words, this is my body and blood, he did not offer them to the women who are with us. Martha said: "He did not offer them to Mary because he saw her laugh."

In their desperation to attack the Magdalene, the fools have admitted both Mary and Martha are at the Last Supper. Mind you it is almost impossible to believe they were not present, as Jesus has been staying every night in their Bethany house for the last five days. So why would they up sticks and go to an empty room in Jerusalem for the Seder. Furthermore it is not a male only event, it is an important family meal.

Look at the order of events leading to the Last Supper in Mark's Gospel.

1. Anointment reclining with Lazarus
2. Judas goes to the Chief Priests
3. The Last Supper reclining with the beloved disciple.

This is the same in Matthew but just before the anointment you get this statement suggesting it is happening during the seven-day Feast of Passover, (Pesach).

'They conspired to arrest Jesus by stealth and kill him. But they said, "Not during the festival, or there may be a riot among the people". (Matthew 26:3)

So it is Passover when the anointing takes place. The first day of the festival is the Seder meal. This clearly suggests the anointing took place at the Last Supper in Bethany and either Jesus is reclining with Lazarus at a lot of suppers, or there is only one, the 'Last Supper' with a lot more people present than usually depicted.

This image in the Magdalene church in Alicante even looks like the Last Supper with the Magdalene wiping Jesus feet with her hair while the disciples sit at the table suggesting this is the Seder meal.

And here are the requirements for the meal:

'When drinking the four cups of wine, and eating the matzot, the korech sandwich, and the afikoman, one is required to recline on a couch, an armchair, or on pillows. This is how royalty and nobility used to eat and on this night the people of Israel are entitled to conduct themselves like royalty.'

And the famous Jewish philosopher, Maimonides writes:

'One is required to see himself as if he had just now left Egyptian slavery. Hence, when a person eats on this night, he

is required to eat and drink while reclining, as a sign of freedom.'

Maimonides adds:

'In the manner that kings and important people eat. When reclining, one should lean to the left, eating and drinking with the right hand. Even one who is left-handed should follow this practice.'

This is why the word reclining is used at both the anointing and the Last Supper. They are clearly the same event with Lazarus reclining with Jesus. By the way you may know Maimonides from this famous quote:

'Give a man a fish and you feed him for a day; teach a man to fish and you feed him for a lifetime.'

But for us he makes a more interesting statement:

'Do not consider it proof just because it is written in books, for a liar who will deceive with his tongue will not hesitate to do the same with his pen.'

I wonder if Maimonides had Luke in mind?

Let me tell the story how I see it, but remember this is un-provable it is just speculation by me, but it must be considered if we are investigating Bethany. The following event, I believe, is happening the day before Passover.

'Martha had a sister called Mary, who sat at the Lord's feet listening. But Martha was distracted by all the preparations that had to be made. She came to him and asked, "Lord, don't you care that my sister has left me to do the work by myself? Tell her to help me!" (Luke 10:38)

'All the preparations that had to be made' does not sound like doing the washing up. It sounds to me like the preparations for the Passover meal, which not only involves preparing all the various symbolic dishes, but cleaning the house, making it absolutely spotless to remove all trace of yeast.

An interesting point about this quote is that Luke who says he has no original information about Jesus is writing this. So where did he get it from? It looks exactly like something coming from John's Gospel. John is often dated late because it was added late to the Bible, but this suggests that John was written before Luke.

The next day at Bethany the meal begins with Jesus washing the feet of his disciples before he reclines down on the couch with Lazarus. Mary Magdalene brings a jar of perfume and she wipes Jesus feet with it. They eat the meal and after we get this:

'When Judas had taken the bread, he went out. And it was night.' (John 13:30)

Strangely, turn the page and we have this:

'Judas (not Iscariot) said to him, "Lord, how is it that you will reveal yourself to us, and not to the world?" (John 14:22)

Another Judas? Who could it be since we are given the names of the disciples in Matthew and there is only one Judas, the one who betrays him? Something has happened that is vitally important because they have accidentally left in the Bible the name of someone who has been cut everywhere else. You will be able to work out for yourselves, the astonishing truth of who this second Judas actually is once you have all the information.

After the meal and the singing of the Passover hymns (Hallel Psalms) they go out into the garden, to an olive pressing area, which is the meaning of the word

Gethsemane. Jesus goes off with Lazarus dressed in a linen cloth which suggests a ritual of some sort.

Judas returns to the garden in Bethany, (not to the room in Jerusalem) with Temple guards and arrests Jesus and Lazarus flees.

When they seized him, he fled naked, leaving his garment behind.' (Mark 14:51)

The Temple Guards take Jesus to the High Priest Annas but they are followed:

'Simon Peter was following Jesus, and so was another disciple. Now that disciple was known to the high priest, and entered with Jesus into the court of the high priest, but Peter was standing at the door outside. So the other disciple, who was known to the high priest, went out and spoke to the doorkeeper, and brought Peter in.'

This is quite extraordinary as the High Priest is one of the most important people in Israel, yet one of Jesus followers has free run of his Palace.

'The chief priests assembled in the palace of the high priest. (Matthew 26:3)

This is like me wandering around Buckingham Palace. It is so weird I think it has to be true and I can only think of one person amongst Jesus' entourage who could be wandering in and out of the High Priests house, and that is the wealthy local boy, Lazarus. This suggests the family of Mary Magdalene were close to being nobility and we should bear that possibility in mind when we follow their story.

That is every possible interpretation of the events accepted as occurring in Bethany, plus the Last Supper, which I speculated probably, occurred in Bethany. You may or may not agree with that, but at least all the possible events are listed. What we have discovered is that, besides the slandering of the Magdalene the early church for some reason does not like any of the people who live in Bethany and this is most pronounced in Luke's Gospel. I have also presented some evidence that Lazarus is the *'disciple Jesus loved'* and I have suggested that his rising from the grave was a death and resurrection ritual. Furthermore it appears Jesus is a hierophant, initiating followers into hidden knowledge very like Pythagoras who Josephus says was very popular in Israel at the time, especially amongst the Essenes who were also known as healers. The Essenes like the Cathars and the Templars all practiced initiations into higher levels of knowledge. Could this be significant because in AD 385 the first person ever to be killed as a heretic was Pricillian, the Christian Bishop of Avila who also believed in levels of initiation? Can this simple belief line you up for extermination?

Chapter Six

THE KNIGHTS TEMPLAR

Are we getting any closer to the reason why the Templars, who swore allegiance to Bethany were tortured and burnt at the stake? To bridge the gap between these twelfth century French Knights and this first century Jerusalem family we need to look into the history of the Knights Templar and their heretical beliefs. But the big problem is that the history books are full of either misunderstandings or misinformation. I will quote you from the encyclopedia Britannica and then explain where they are wrong.

'Following the success of the First Crusade (1095–99) most Crusaders returned home after fulfilling their vows, and Christian pilgrims to Jerusalem suffered attacks from Muslim raiders. Pitying the plight of these Christians, eight or nine French knights led by Hugh de Payns vowed in late 1119 or early 1120 to devote themselves to the pilgrims' protection and to form a religious community for that purpose. Baldwin II, king of Jerusalem, gave them quarters in a wing of the royal palace in the area of the former Temple of Solomon, and from this they derived their name.' (Britannica)

The truth is there is no report about these nine knights who went to Jerusalem in 1118 to protect pilgrims, till it was written by Guillaume de Tyre about sixty years later in 1180 when they were all dead. Nobody mentions them even being in Jerusalem. In fact the suggested reason they went to Jerusalem looks more like a miss-direction than anything else, because there were only nine Knights for the first nine years so how could they even guard the one road from the sea to Jerusalem on horseback, a forty-mile stretch. They could easily be ambushed themselves by Moslem brigands. It is clearly nonsense. What we know from Freemason ritual is that they were in fact excavating under the Temple. Below Old Jerusalem is a network of tunnels build to conceal precious objects and holy artifacts in case of invasion. In 1952 in a cave near where the Dead Sea Scrolls were found, archeologists discovered two Copper Scrolls, which list sacred objects and treasure hidden in over sixty sites. Here is an example:

"In the old burial cave of Beit Ḥemdah on the third stratum, there are sixty-five golden ingots."

And:

"Between the two houses that are in the Valley of Achor, in their very midst, buried to a depth of three cubits, there are two pots full of silver."

Sixty-three sites are listed and the treasure of gold and silver has been estimated in the tons. The sixty-fourth and final listing does not list treasure but points to a duplicate document with additional details. Significantly that document has never been found. Could that have been in the hands of the excavating Knights?

There is a story told by Josephus about the tunnels under Temple mound. Soon after the Roman destruction of Jerusalem:

'Simon bar Giora imagining that he could cheat the Romans by creating a scare, dressed himself in a white tunics and buckling over them a purple mantle arose out of the ground at the very spot whereon the Temple formerly stood. The spectators were at first aghast and remained motionless.'

Sadly it did not work, Simon was sent to Rome in chains and furthermore Josephus tells us that:

'His emergence from the ground led to the discovery of a large number of other rebels in subterranean passages.'

 In fact a British Army excavation under Temple Mound found part of a Templar sword, a spur, the remains of a lance and a small Templar cross. These artifacts are suspiciously held by Robert Brydon, the Templar archivist for Scotland, whose grandfather was a friend of one of the British excavators. I say suspiciously, because it makes me wonder if this British Army excavation was instigated by Freemasons?

If the Templars were guarding the roads in Palestine, why on there return to France did their patron and protector, St. Bernard de Clairvaux write:

'The work has been accomplished with our help, and the Knights have been sent on a journey through France and Burgundy, under the protection of the Count of Champaign, where all precautions can be taken against interference by public or ecclesiastical authority.'

What work has been accomplished? Pilgrims were still visiting Jerusalem! So can we take it for granted that the Templars found what they were looking for, precious items, treasure and scrolls that contained heretical information that needed to be kept out of the hands of the ecclesiastical authorities? That the Templars became rich and powerful clearly answers that question.

Some speculate the Knights were looking for the Ark of the Covenant others the Holy Grail and others important scrolls. Here for instance, the French historian Gaetan Delaforge wrote:

'The real task of the nine Knights was to carry out research in the area in order to obtain certain relics and manuscripts which contain the essence of the secret traditions of Judaism and ancient Egypt, some probably went back to the days of Moses.'

Certainly in this tracing board belonging to Royal Arch Freemasons we see a chamber located below the ruins of Solomon's Temple.

Notice the shields of the twelve tribes of Israel and the scattered Masonic implements. Special to Royal Arch are not the usual Masonic building implements, compass and set-square etc. but excavating tools, pick-axe, shovel and crowbar, shown here with the discovered scroll and all before the triple Tao, which we will deal with later.

So perhaps Delaforge is a Royal Arch Mason, which is why he suggests they searched for scrolls. While the nine knights may have found very important ancient scrolls that was not the main aim of the excavation, it was clearly the gold and the silver deposited.

In 1962, archeologist John Allegro led an expedition that investigated several possible burial places but nothing was ever found. So clearly the knights found what they were looking for and took it to France.

Perhaps when Guillaume de Tyre wrote his account of the Templars in 1180, the many recruits who had joined after the Templars were made official in 1129 were in fact employed to guard the roads, so that he assumed that was their original purpose, which has then be copied by historians who would have no other original source.

The main question that arises is, did the original knights have a copper scroll or the information contained in it? If so where did they get it from? Surely they were not excavating for nine years just on the slight possibility that there might be treasure to be found. If so why did nobody else dig down for it, since it was placed there a thousand years earlier when the Roman's invaded in 69 AD? But let us return to the encyclopedia Britannica

The Templars obtained further sanction at the Council of Troyes in 1128, which may have requested that Bernard of Clairvaux compose the new rule. Bernard also wrote In Praise

We need to understand who this cleric Bernard of Clairvaux is and what his role was in drawing up the Templar's rules and singing their praises.

Remember Bernard has already mentioned an important contact of his when writing about the return of the nine knights to France:

"under the protection of the Count of Champagn, where all precautions can be taken against interference by public or ecclesiastical authority.'

The Count of Champagn was exceedingly rich and powerful and it is worth listing the activities of the Count as it gives us several dates that help our investigation. We know that after the capture of Jerusalem in 1099 the Count attended a meeting in France of several important families including Andre de Montbard who became the fifth Grand Master of the Temple.

Following this in 1104 the Count of Champagne left for the Holy Land with an associate of Montbard.
In 1112 Andre de Montbard's nephew, young Saint Bernard, to everybody's surprised, joined the almost defunct Cistercians.
In 1114 the Count of Champagn departed on a second journey to the Holy Land.
In 1115 he returned and donated land to Saint Bernard for the Abbey of Clairvaux after which the Cistercians seemed to become rich and famous. Bernard clearly was sponsored by Champagn to be a mouthpiece for the Templars.

Remember this is all happening prior to the arrival of the nine excavating knights in Jerusalem in 1118. So the Count is making trips to the Holy Land and financing the Templar mouthpiece, Saint Bernard all before the nine knights arrived in Jerusalem, so you can decide what year the Templars were formed either on the arrival of the nine Knights or before. Or could it actually have been as late as 1128 because, as mentioned in Britannica, at the Church Council convened in Troyes, the Templars were officially incorporated as a religious-military order, and there the rules of conduct were drawn up by Saint Bernard. So no rules existed before then so was there no organization before then?

Yet again, Troyes where the Church Council convened, was the seat of the court of the Count of Champagn and interestingly it was Chrétian of Troyes who wrote one of the earliest Grail romances, which figured the Templars as the guardians of the Grail. I should add that the Count made Troyes, a centre of Cabalistic and esoteric studies as early as 1070. Central to this was a Rabbi probably known even today by Orthodox Jews as Solomon of Troyes, or Rabbi Rashid. Rashid was author of a comprehensive commentary on the Talmud, which has been included in every edition of the Talmud since its first printing in the 1520s. It must also be obvious that the people who would know what was under the Jerusalem Temple would be Israelites.

André de Montbard who was uncle to Saint Bernard de Clairvaux was a vassal of the Count of Champagne. He entered the Order in 1119 and became second-in-command to the Grand Master. He died in Jerusalem on 17 January 1156 and was succeeded by Cathar sympathizer, Bertrand de Blanchefort who conferred on the Templars land in the environs of Bézu, near Rennes-le-Château. Bertrand notably used German miners to secretly excavate in his lands and some believe it was to conceal precious objects found in Jerusalem. He built around him a body of Knights possibly to protect the cache. The same suspect story of protecting Pilgrims on the road was used to explain their activity in Bézu. But this was even more ridiculous than the original, as the roads he was protecting were 'El Camino' to Santiago de Compostela a thousand miles away! Marie de Blanchefort's encoded gravestone in the church of Rennes-le-Château began the famous mystery that spawned the best sellers, *Holy Blood Holy Grail* and *The Da Vinci Code*. Returning to the encyclopedia we get this mistake:

'The Knights Templar swore an oath of poverty, chastity, and obedience.'

In fact the original Latin translates as *'chastity, obedience and to hold all property in common'*. Clearly there is nothing there about poverty at all. So our first question is who are they swearing obedience to? And secondly, whom are they going to hold property and wealth in common with? Obviously the Count of Champagn is one obvious candidate. Another is the financier of the excavations, Fulk d' Anjou who would became King of Jerusalem in 1131. He visited Jerusalem while the excavations were underway and gave a financial annuity to the Knights to continue their work before returning to Anjou. The Anjou family figure massively in our story.

One must bear in mind something that Eliphas Levi wrote about the Templars that suggests a possible hidden agenda that we will be dealing with later:

'The Chiefs alone knew whither they were going;
the rest followed unsuspectingly.' (Eliphas Levi)

Chapter Seven

NOTRE DAME

There is a lot more incredible miss-information about the Templars and their demise that has spawned lots of crazy theories. I like this from Umberto Eco:

'You can tell a lunatic by the liberties he takes with common sense, by his flashes of inspiration, and by the fact that sooner or later he brings up the Templars.' (Foucault's Pendulum)

I must admit I am quite worried about the actual information I have about the Templars, because if I put it in print, people might think I am a lunatic. But for now I am just going to deal with one last massive mistake in the encyclopedia's description of the Templars that is, I am afraid to say, accepted by all academic scholars. Here it is in the Encyclopedia Britannica:

'The Templars 'expressed particular veneration to the Virgin Mary.' (Britannica)

And the same is repeated in the many books.

'The Virgin Mary was their patroness and protector, and novices were told that 'we were established in honor of our Lady.' (Secrets of the Knights Templar)

No, the person they *'were established in honor of...'* was not the Virgin Mother. 'Our Lady' of course in French is Notre Dame and it is Notre Dame who they venerated not the Virgin Mother. Now you are obviously as confused as everybody else because you think Notre Dame is the 'Virgin Mary'. But I am afraid the Church has pulled the wool over everybody on this one. Notre Dame originally was Mary Magdalene! The designation was removed by the church from the Magdalene and attached to the virgin mother, and a whole new cult was manufactured around the mother by Rome in another attempt to play down the Magdalene.

It is surprising that the books talk about the Templars venerating the Virgin Mother, mistaking her for the person titled Notre Dame, as not only does the Templar rule state that Mary Magdalene should be venerated and her feast day of the 22nd July was openly and legitimately recognized in their calendar. Even after their arrest, one of the charges against the Templars was worshipping Mary Magdalene. Furthermore although the Templars were not active in the first crusade, the Second was deliberately launched by Pope Eugenius (one of Bernard of Clarvaux's Cistercian monks) from the Church of Mary Magdalene at Vézelay, as it was believed to contain Mary Magdalene's bones.

It is absolutely clear that the Templars never venerated the Virgin Mary, because one of the crimes leveled against them at their trials was that they did not accept the Virgin Mary's status. But the mistake continues in all the books. Here is a description of Templar initiation.

'The postulant simply knelt with his hand on a Bible, declaring his obeisance to God, the Virgin Mary and the Templar Rule.' (Secrets of the Knights Templar)

Why state this when it is immediately followed by.

'But this has never been completely established.'

So why invent what occurred at initiation? It was held in secret with dreadful threats against anyone revealing the ceremony. Certainly the church succeeded in fooling the whole academic community on this one.

Churches built to Notre Dame during the height of the Templars in the 12th century were all dedicated to Mary Magdalene. It is obvious, the masons building Notre Dame de Paris knew very well who they were building it for. The man responsible for the building of Notre Dame in 1163 was the Bishop of Paris, Maurice de Sully. His history shows links to the beliefs of the Templars who were just rising to their heights. For instance he converted a synagogue that was seized from the Jews of Paris, and duly consecrated it as a church dedicated to Mary Magdalene! So the Magdalene was foremost in his mind, but what about the Virgin Mother? Sully forbade the celebration of her feast of the Immaculate Conception in his diocese. So I think it is clear whom he and the masons actually dedicated Notre Dame to, as did Victor Hugo when he wrote the 'Hunchback of Notre Dame' as he was steeped in the French esoteric world. Remember Quasimodo is elected 'Pope of Fools' at a festival parodying cardinal elections, and is subsequently beaten by an angry mob. And who is the bady in the story, the Catholic, Archdeacon Frollo. Incidentally Victor Hugo also visited Bartholdi's Paris studio to see his Statue of Liberty in production, before it was sent by French Freemasons to their brother Freemasons in America.

On inspection you will find that the Roman Church has, through the centuries, made pronouncements to assert the Virgin Mary's importance, even though she hardly appears in the Gospels. They insist that their invented teachings about her are dogmas of faith. These include belief in her virginal conception of Jesus, taught by the First Council of Nicaea in 325 AD. Then the Second Council of Constantinople in 553 advocated the weird claim of her perpetual virginity. This doctrine of the Immaculate

Conception states that from the first moment of her existence, Mary was without original sin. (Meaning she was born like Jesus, without her parents having sex) This doctrine was proclaimed a dogma ex cathedra by Pope Pius IX in 1854.

The dogma of the Assumption of Mary, defined by Pope Pius XII in 1950, states that, at the end of her earthly life, she rose to heaven, body and soul. Other than the story of God or the Angel Gabriel impregnating Mary the other pronouncements are nothing to do with what is in the Gospels, this is the Church thrusting weird ideas down people's throats as matters of dogma.

I must show you what Leonardo Da Vinci thought of the Immaculate Conception. Leonardo received a brief in 1483 from the Confraternity of the Immaculate Conception, a brotherhood of Franciscan monks, elected to promote the Vatican's weird doctrine. He painted the celebrated '*Virgin of the Rocks*' of which there has been much speculation, but none of it seems to see the obvious.

Look at it and consider what Immaculate Conception is Leonardo talking about in this painting? Study it carefully and ask yourself if it shows God has impregnated this virgin? Okay you don't see it, but am I mad or is that strange rock sticking up in the hole on the right, not the most phallic thing you have ever seen in your life?

And to make sure you don't think it is a mistake, the rocks on the left are in the form of a hand. Is this God's rock hand and rock c...ck? It even looks like it is spurting something. Is this another example of Leonardo's famed sense of humor or is it just my naughty imagination. But if you still don't buy it, at the Virgin's feet in the London version there is another phallic symbol, an Arum Lily, the traditional flower of the bridal bouquet with an exaggerated, erect, male stamen.

Virgin on what rocks?
Expert, Laurence Gardner tells us that the central character in all paintings was never described by Leonardo as the Madonna; he called her La Nostra Signora, Italian for the French, Notre Dame. The term used for Mary Magdalene by the Knights Templar and the Troubadours.

The setting is not the Egyptian desert, so it is not a painting of the Flight to Egypt as sometimes suggested, but a cave in a fertile rocky landscape.

As Leonardo was involved with esoteric ideas, he would have believed that after Mary's time of preaching in Marseilles, she moved to the mountain cave in Sainte-Baume and lived out her days there in prayer and contemplation.

This is the mountainous cave where Mary was alleged to have spent her final years.

Most Magdalene Churches has an image of her final days in the cave in Sainte-Baume. So I think we can safely say that many believe the story of her travel to Gaul and her final days in the cave. Which possibly makes her, Notre Dame of the Rocks?

In 1956 papers were deposited anonymously in the National French archives, about the little church of the Magdalene in Rennes-le-Château, hinting that someone with insider knowledge had deposited them. They give unknown but accurate details of the Templars and also knowledge of the Cathars and the Rosicrucians. Amongst these secret documents is a poem in French called the Serpent Rouge, with each verse relating to a sign of the Zodiac. Leo gives us this:

From she who I desire to liberate, there wafts towards me the fragrance of the perfume, which impregnates the sepulcher. Formerly some named her ISIS, queen of the beneficial spring, COME UNTO ME ALL YE WHO SUFFER AND ARE AFFLICTED, AND I SHALL GIVE YE REST. To others she is MAGDALENE, of the celebrated vase fulled with healing balm. The initiates know her true name: NOTRE DAME DES CROSS.

Somebody clearly had access to insider knowledge and may or may not have added this poem to tease us. But whatever the reason this poem clearly states that those who are initiated know who Notre Dame refers to and it is not the Virgin Mother. By the way the last four words are as they appear in the French, 'Notre Dame des cross' with cross in English not 'croix', which is the French. And cross is singular but 'des' is pleural so it actually should translate as Notre Dame of the crosses! I can only think that the crosses is referring to the double cross of the cross of Lorraine, which was a symbol used by King Rene de Anjou whose family you will remember financed the Templar excavations. I should add here that King Rene had a famous goblet with the words engraved on it:

"Whoever drinks from this shall see God. Whoever drinks it in one draught, will see Mary Magdalene."

Let me tell you a little story, that proves nothing yet but the details will figure later. You have of course heard of the prophesies of Nostradamus but you may not have realized the name is a Latinization of Notre Dame. He was born on 14th December 1503 in Saint-Rémy-de-Provence. He was the son of notary Jaume who worked as a physician. Jaume's family had originally been Jewish, but his father, Cresquas, a grain and money dealer based a few miles north in Avignon, had converted to Catholicism in 1460, taking the Christian name 'Pierre' and the surname 'Nostredame' the saint on whose day his conversion was solemnized. (22nd July?) The earliest ancestor who can be identified on the paternal side is Astruge of Carcassonne, who died about 1420. Our young Nostradamus was Christened, Michel Nortredame but became known as Nostradamus. Here are some points to consider. Firstly, his family were Jewish converts and we must wonder which, Notre Dame a Jew would be commemorating, Mary Magdalene famously loved and venerated in this area of France by the Jews, or the Virgin Mother? Secondly his grandfather lived in Carcassonne the centre of Catharism that the Roman Church in 1209, launched a Crusade against that lasted twenty years and wiped out most of the local population. His father worked in Avignon where the Romanesque church of Notre Dame des Doms was built way back in 1150. This Magdalene church was abandoned and allowed to deteriorate, but then was renovated in 1840. A new bell tower was erected in 1859 and placed on top is a massive gilded statue of the Virgin Mary. Is she or is she not Notre Dame des Doms that is the question? Anyway I hope you will again forgive the digression, which offers people, places and actions that you will begin to recognize as they keep re-appearing in our analysis.

I recommend a visit to another Notre Dame Cathedral, recognized as the height of the medieval Masons art. Notre Dame d'Chartres noted for its much-celebrated original stained glass windows. The Magdalene window has panels that depict all the events in her life. And like all Magdalene churches it totally ignores all the huffing and puffing by officialdom and makes the Magdalene the sister of Lazarus and the person who perfumes Jesus' feet. And therefore drives a massive hole in the invention of a Mary of Bethany.

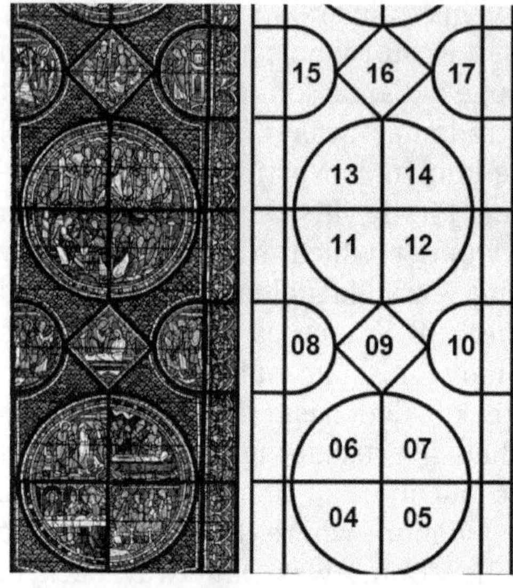

Some of the panels are of real interest to us. Here is one panel that shows the Magdalene stepping off a boat.

There is no story in the Bible that tells us about a journey the Magdalene took. Where has she traveled to? And who is this person, dressed as a bishop, preaching in the Magdalene window? How does he relate to the Magdalene?

And like in most Magdalene churches you get an image of the Magdalene in a cave with a skull. This is a version from the altar of the Church at Rennes-le-Château painted by the famous priest, Sauniére himself.

I must confess that I was very disheartened that the big Magdalene Church in Paris has no images of the Magdalene doing anything, neither the anointing or raising Lazarus or anything else, as if it was wiped clean of her story. But not to be too depressed the Church in Alicante has the lot, the anointing, the raising of Lazarus and like Saunière's painting, the cave and skull in pride of place behind the altar.

To understand these images we have to go back to Israel and Josephus' description of the build up to the war with Rome.

Chapter Eight

WAR CLOUDS

This is actually the heading of a chapter in Josephus book, *'The Jewish War'* and I have re-used it as most of the information in this chapter comes directly from his chapter.

Like any society, Israel had its aristocracy and plebeians, its rich and its poor. There were three types of Aristocracy, Herod the Great's family and their descendants. Then those descended from Judas Maccabee who made himself king after defeating the Greek administration 150 years earlier. And those who could trace their family tree back to David. The Jewish ancestral records of these family trees were considered important enough for the Romans to issue instructions to destroy them.

Now look at one of the earliest actions of the war, which shows that this was more than a war against the Romans, it was actually a revolution.

'The king's troops, inferior now in numbers as well as courage, were driven out of the Upper City. Their opponents rushed in and burnt down the house of Ananias, the High Priest and the palace of Agrippa and Berenice; then they took their fire to the records office, eager to destroy the money lenders' bonds and so make impossible the recovery of debts, in order to secure the support of an army of debtors and enable the poor to rise with impunity against the rich.' (Josephus, 'War')

So like many National liberation struggles, this war seems to have snowballed into a Communist revolution against the ruling class. This was true of the Vietnamese fight against the Japanese, which led to communist, Ho Chi Min becoming the leader. So can one say the events of 66 AD were the first Communist revolution since many participants believed in the idea of living in communes? This is certainly true of the followers of Jesus as shown in Acts of the Apostles.

'All the believers were one in heart and mind. No one claimed that any of their possessions was their own, but they shared everything they had.' (Acts 4:32)

Now Josephus reports that around 40 AD Israel was plunged into strife and catastrophe and clearly became a place where the rich and aristocracy were in much danger. Their homes were burnt, their livestock stolen, debts were clearly not going to be paid now the records office was destroyed. They must have been leaving Israel in droves and buying estates abroad. Many would have gone to Egypt, especially Alexandria where there was a large Jewish population. Others went to Iraq, Syria and even India where the Bene Israeli live.

But it looks like the very rich and the aristocracy traveled much further afield. They sailed west to the other end of the Mediterranean, to Gaul where we certainly know the Herodian royalty had estates. We have written evidence that there was a huge quantity of Jews in the area of the Narbonne by 600 AD as Archbishop Julian of Toledo described the region as *'a brothel of blaspheming Jews.'*

Two hundred years later this same area called Septimania was given over to these Jews for helping the

Frankish King, Pepin III to defeat the Moslems. So a Jewish Kingdom was established, which crossed the border of France and Spain around Narbonne. We have clear evidence that this western migration was normal for the rich who could afford such a journey and clearly we are talking about huge numbers as Jerusalem was absolutely flattened by the Romans.

There is a mass of evidence for such a migration even to a book on Alchemy that Nicholas Flamel (1330-1418) claims he found:

'The book contained thrice seven leaves, so numbered at the top of each folio, every seventh leaf having painted images and figures instead of writing. On the first written leaf the following words were inscribed in great characters of gold, "Abraham the Jew, Prince, Priest, Levite, Astrologer and Philosopher, unto the tribe of the Jews who by the wrath of God, were dispersed amongst the Gauls." The person who sold me this book must have not known its value. My suspicion is that it was either stolen from the miserable Jews or found hidden somewhere in the old place of their abode.'

This migration of Jews is even mentioned in the 20th degree of Freemasonry known as the 'Grand Master'. The degree tells of the destruction of the third Temple by Titus in AD 70 and how the Brethren, sadly left the Holy Land and divided themselves into a number of lodges and dispersed around Europe.

Now consider this migration, which began with the list of troubles Josephus mentioned from around 42 AD, just a few years after the death of Jesus. These Jews would clearly know the story of Jesus and his famous brother James was still there preaching and still praying for atonement at the

Temple till his death in 62 AD. They would know all the stories sold to the Romans by Paul were very odd to say the least, because these Jews were not uneducated peasants. An English monk, Theobald of Cambridge, wrote:

'The chief men and rabbis of the Jews who dwell in Spain assembled together at Narbonne, where the Royal Seed resides, and where they are held in the highest esteem.'

These are clearly well educated men including rabbi and even Royal Princes.

Could a rich Jewish family from Bethany have made this same journey to Gaul and is this the missing link we have been searching for between Bethany, Notre Dame and the French Knights Templar?

Chapter Nine

THE VOYAGE

There is a lot of circumstantial evidence that one particularly rich family, who had all the insider information about Jesus, made the journey from their large house in Bethany to the Jewish community in Gaul. Tradition has it that Mary Magdalene, Martha and Lazarus and Maximin set sail around 43 AD to escape persecution and this would seem very likely since the Sanhedrin had deemed Jesus a blasphemer and had him killed, so any of his direct followers would be under suspicion. In fact the Bible states that Peter was arrested and brought before the Sanhedrin. It is suggested by some that our rich family left Israel by boat, others that they traveled to Alexandria from where they set sail for Marseilles.

In the boat with the Magdalene were Martha, Lazarus and Maximin, alleged to be one of the seventy-two disciples mentioned in Acts. During a storm at sea the boat was blown sixty miles off course and finally came to shore west of their destination on the coast of the Camargue.

The following painting depicts the legend that the Queen of Marseilles welcomed Mary Magdalene, an unlikely event but it certainly is entrenched in the area that the Magdalene did arrive there.

Now in case you doubt my assertion that Notre Dame was the Magdalene and not the Virgin Mother, let me tell you about the town that according to longstanding tradition, the boat landed with the Bethany family. I say tradition as opposed to legend because this is an oral transmission, from generation to generation, facts really rooted in the history. The developing town and church was called Notre-

Dame-de-la-Barque and during Templar times became Notre-Dame-de-la-Mer. The usual attack on the Magdalene is clear here. This town should be one of the most Holy sites in Christendom. But is it? Not at all, it is a small seaside resort with a fairground. Every attempt has been made to downplay it.

Suddenly the Bethany family are not in the boat but instead there were three Maries, Mary Magdalene, Mary Jacob and Mary Salome and even the servant Sara but none of the others. Where is Martha and Lazarus and Maximin; and where did these others come from? This looks exactly like the same tactic used during the resurrection of Jesus to downplay the Magdalene.

In John's Gospel Mary Magdalene is alone when she discovers the empty tomb and then meets Jesus and mistakes him for the gardener:

'Early on the first day of the week, while it was still dark, Mary Magdalene went to the tomb and saw that the stone had been removed from the entrance.'

But now look at the synoptic Gospels, which were the original Bible, starting with Mark:

'When the Sabbath was over, Mary Magdalene, Mary the mother of James, and Salome bought spices so that they might go to anoint Jesus' body. Very early on the first day of the week, just after sunrise, they were on their way to the tomb and they asked each other, 'Who will roll the stone away from the entrance of the tomb?' But when they looked up, they saw that the stone, which was very large, had been rolled away.'

Now what reason could there be for adding these others? These are the same people added to the landing place of the

Magdalene. Is it an accident or the same tactic used in Notre Dame-de-la-Mer. Add others to remove the importance of the Magdalene. Of course we know who is going to remove the Magdalene totally. Luke of course:

'On the first day of the week, very early in the morning, the women took the spices they had prepared and went to the tomb. They found the stone rolled away from the tomb.'(24:1)

Unlike Luke, Matthew has no problem with the names but still has another woman present. And also has a rather dramatic version of rolling the stone away:

After the Sabbath, at dawn on the first day of the week, Mary Magdalene and the other Mary went to look at the tomb. There was a violent earthquake, for an angel of the Lord came down from heaven and, going to the tomb, rolled back the stone and sat on it.'

I am not sure how these witness statements about the resurrection would stand up in a court of law, with the stone door closed – or the stone door open! There is one women – or there are two women – or there are three women! There is one angel sitting on the stone – or there is one angel inside – or there are two angels outside! I know who I believe, but that is another story. For now let us return to the landing place of Mary Magdalene.

After adding these extra Maries they then changed the name from Notre Dame-de-la-Mer to the awkward, Saintes-Maries-de-la-Mer, to reflect the other Maries, and to disassociate Mary Magdalene from the name Notre Dame.
Now they made a concerted effort to even disassociate the Magdalene completely from the site. From the three Maries you can now see that the statue in the church has only two!

Which Mary is missing from this tableau? Why the Magdalene of course! A town and a church dedicated to her landing has had her removed. I could not believe my eyes and in the tourist shop outside I resented paying three Euros but I had to buy this postcard of the outrage. See it says, Mary Jacob and Mary Salome and even the servant Sara, but no Mary Magdalene!

The actual original name was Notre Dame de-la-Mer not mentioning the other Maries at all but now we have the other Maries but no Mary Magdalene. I have my doubts that the other Maries were ever in the boat as other sources don't give them as traveling companions.

They have no shame, changing the name of the town and removing the Magdalene from the boat. What is strange is that one of the remaining images in the boat is probably Mary Magdalene with her red hair and her jar at her feet. I wonder if the locals, when they were told to remove Mary Magdalene, removed one of the others in defiance. If they did, well done you guys, for that you deserve a Navette.

Navettes are French cookies from Marseilles that are shaped like a boat to commemorate Mary Magdalene and Martha and their voyage to Marseilles. Despite the church they keep that story alive any way they can.

One interesting feature of the postcard is the inclusion of the statuette of Sara , the supposed Egyptian servant who is venerated by the Gypsy horsemen of the Camargue.

Every May 24 the Roma take Sara down to the sea from where she came. Now I have grave doubts that this statue was of their servant. I think this is one of the many black Madonnas that appear in this very area where the

Magdalene lived and preached. So one assumes these are statuettes of Mary Magdalene. So one suspects Sara is the real image of the Magdalene and those Europeans in the boat are church fakes. I have reminded you already that the Magdalene was born a Jew and died a Jew, and now I would suggest like most original Israelites she was black. Geneticists have discovered that the purest surviving remnant of the Children of Israel identified by CMH tests is the tribe of Black Jews in India. The Bene Israel and the Black Jews of Cochin, who show a genetic affinity not only to Ethiopians and Yemenites, but also to the tribe of Black Jews in South Africa, the Lemba, whose relation to the ancient Hebrews has also been confirmed by the presence of high frequencies of the CMH. Thus, genetics confirms that the ancient Hebrews were black.

You can see that in the earliest image of Peter and Paul they have black features, but in the later one they have given them Roman noses and wavy hair. And you will find in images now they are totally Europeanized.

 Genetics has thrown up some very interesting origins for populations, but one of the most controversial is that the Palestinians in Israel are not Arabs but are actually Israelites who converted to Islam after they were freed from the Byzantine Empire, because if you converted you did not have to pay tax. And then surprisingly the Ashkenazi Jews who are arriving in Israel have been shown to be genetically related, not to Semites, but to Kurds, Turks and East Europeans. They were in fact Kazars from central Europe who converted to Judaism and not Israelites at all. I better stop here as this information is disliked both by the Ashkenazi Jews and the Palestinian Moslems. Pity.

When I was in Notre Dame-de-la-Mer, all I saw was a small plaque celebrating the visit of Pope John 23 to the town. No massive celebration of this Holy site, just the one good Pope John 23 who broke all the rules and who, insider Malachi Martin suggests was a secret Freemason; this is the only visiting modern Pope.

Local legend has it that Martha traveled towards Avignon and ended up in Tarascon where she lived and died and is buried there in St Martha's Church. Mary Magdalene, Lazarus and Maximin traveled on to Marseille, where Mary Magdalene began to preach and Lazarus became the first bishop of Marseille.

The Magdalene then went on to Aix with Maximin who become the first bishop of Aix and it is he who is pictured in the Magdalene window in Notre-Dame-de Chartres.

Mary Magdalene later left him to continue his apostolate alone and she withdrew to the solitude of a cave now called La Sainte-Baume.

So this is the cave in France depicted in Mary Magdalene churches.

On the day she knew she was to die she descended into the plain and died in the arms of Maximin so one suspects he was her lover, which is why he traveled with the Bethany family. But that may be objected to by those who make Mary Magdalene Jesus wife.

The skull of Lazarus is in a reliquary at Cathedral of Saint Mary Major in Marseille. Mary Magdalene died around 62 AD and her body was laid in an alabaster sarcophagus in an oratory Maximin constructed in the Roman town of Villa

Latta, which after Maximin's death became St. Maximin. In 710 AD her body was transferred and buried in a marble tomb so that the Saracens could not find it. In 1279 Charles II of Anjou excavated and the marble tomb was re-discovered. In the dust inside the tomb was a wooden tablet wrapped in wax declaring: "Here lies the body of Mary Magdalene". Inside was a parchment, which explained the move in 710.

Today the skull of Saint Mary Magdalene is in a gold reliquary in the Basilica of Saint Mary Magdalene in the town of St. Maximin-la-Sainte-Baume. Perhaps this is the head the Templars were accused of venerating as Baphomet: baphomet being the code for Sophia, which translates as feminine wisdom.

That is the story as told in France, obviously with more information than I have written, and it usually finishes with the Magdalene having converted everybody in the Languedoc to Christianity.

There are more details to this story and I am sure if you were to make a tour of the area, reading the history of each stop, everything would fall into place.

Start at the heretical church of Rennes-le-Château, and to the amazing castle at Carcassonne the stronghold of the Cathars. Then to Narbonne, *a brothel of blaspheming Jews*. And on to Bishop Maximin's Aix-en-Provence and to the right is the cave, Saint Baume. Not far is Martha's Tarascon, below it on the coast the landing place Notre-Dame-de-la-Mer. To the right is Bishop Lazarus' Marseille. I would end such a tour at Nimes where there is a Roman Amphitheater still in use as a bullfighting arena, and up the road to the amazing walled town of Avignon with its Papal Palace where seven successive Popes resided. It is an amazing trip and you will get some amazing photos.

RENNES-LE-CHÂTEAU
Here the ex-wife also torments Asmodeus who guards the door
of the mysterious Mary Magdalene church at Rennes-le-Château

Chapter Ten

CONVERSION

A really odd part of this story is the supposed conversion of the people of the Languedoc to Christianity by the Magdalene. Firstly, the area where the Magdalene landed was occupied by hundreds, if not thousands of Jewish families who had left Israel during the troubles. Secondly, Mary Magdalene, like Jesus were born and died as Jews, so who was the Magdalene converting in 50 AD, and to what? She is a Jew preaching to Jews. Christianity was not yet invented as Paul had not yet arrived in Rome, and when he did in 62 AD his first act was to visit a synagogue:

'When they had assembled, Paul said to them: "My brothers, although I have done nothing against our people or against the customs of our ancestors, I was arrested in Jerusalem…. They replied, "We have not received any letters from Judea concerning you…. He witnessed to them from morning till evening, he tried to persuade them about Jesus. Some were convinced by what he said, but others would not believe. They began to leave after Paul had made this final statement: "The Holy Spirit spoke the truth to your ancestors when he said through Isaiah: "You will be ever hearing but never understanding; you will be ever seeing but never perceiving." For this people's heart has become calloused.' "Therefore I want you to know that God's salvation has been sent to the Gentiles, and they will listen!" (Acts 28:23)

So Paul preached to Jews with his version of the Jesus story, but when they rejected him he turned to the Gentiles who would be followers of the Roman pantheon of Gods, and who often made Gods of their important Emperors. For instance Julius Caesar was made a God and we get the month July from him, and Augustus was made a God and we get the month of August from this God. So for Gentiles, making Jesus a God is no big deal but to Jews....!

But what about the Magdalene and Lazarus, they were also Jews preaching to Jews around 50 AD, presumably in synagogues, about the life and ideas of Jesus who had died just a dozen years earlier. But why, unlike Paul, were they successful? Was it because they knew Jesus personally while Paul had no real insights about what Jesus really taught? Paul was certainly trying to sell ideas that were very un-Jewish.

'At once he began to preach in the synagogues that Jesus is the Son of God.' (Acts 9:20)

This surely would be blasphemous to Jews who are very strongly monotheists and could accept Jesus as a great Prophet but not as the Son of God. On top of this he adds that Jesus raised people from the dead, and Paul even claimed he himself had raised the dead.

'Seated in a window was a young man named Eutychus, who was sinking into a deep sleep as Paul talked on and on. When he was sound asleep, he fell to the ground from the third story and was picked up dead. Paul went down, threw himself on the young man and put his arms around him. "Don't be alarmed," he said. "He's alive!" Then he went upstairs again and broke bread and ate.' (Acts 20:9)

I must admit this is one of my favorite moments in the New Testament; Paul bores this young man to death and then resurrects him. But he continues with more un-Jewish activity:

'For I received from the Lord what I also passed on to you: the Lord Jesus, on the night he was betrayed, took bread, and when he had given thanks, he broke it and said, 'This is my body, which is for you; do this in remembrance of me.' In the same way, after supper he took the cup, saying, 'This cup is the new covenant in my blood; do this, whenever you drink it, in remembrance of me.' For whenever you eat this bread and drink this cup, you proclaim the Lord's death until he comes. (1 Corinthians 11:23)

Now what Paul is saying is that although he never met Jesus, he has formed his ideas from a personal supernatural visit by Jesus. Then in a very un-Jewish way he is the first to introduce the idea that eating bread and drinking blood at the Passover meal, something that even symbolically would be disgusting to a Jew. Just listen to this from Justin Martyr a second century Christian father.

'When Jesus said, "drink this wine, this is my blood," he gave this ritual to them alone, yet the wicked demons in imitation, in the Mysteries of Mithras also delivered the command to do so.' (Justin Martyr)

What he is complaining about is that in an earlier religion, the Mysteries of Mithras, initiates were offered a sacrament of water mixed with wine and a wafer bearing the sign of a cross. And of course there's this:

You may think this is Jesus but in fact it is the Mystery god-man 'Mithras'. As Paul comes from the Mithras centre of Tarsus, this is probably why the idea has popped into his head and however genuinely he believes it is Jesus' spirit talking to him, I think he is fooling himself because this is clearly from Mithras. Even when Paul turns to the Gentiles he upsets the Jews by saying you don't have to be circumcised or eat kosher food to follow the Jewish God. So I am not surprised the Jews rejected Paul and in fact when he tried to enter the Temple in Jerusalem there was a riot.

Now we have to ask, what were Lazarus and the Magdalene teaching to the Jews of Gaul that they seem to have accepted their philosophies? Obviously Lazarus would not be teaching that he was raised from the dead, just as you would never hear any third degree Freemason admitting that he was raised from the dead. This is a secret ritual to be played out to the surprise of the novitiate during initiation.

Perhaps the letter from Clement of Alexandria will give us a real clue about the beliefs of Jesus.

"Mark went to Alexandria, bringing both his knowledge and the things he remembered hearing from Peter. He arranged a more spiritual gospel for the use of those being perfected. Nevertheless, he did not reveal the things, which are not to be discussed. He did not write out the hierophantic instruction of the Lord. Then, he added certain sayings, the interpretation of which he knew would initiate the hearers into the innermost sanctuary of the truth which has been hidden

seven times. And when he died, he left his writing to the church in Alexandria, where it is even now still extremely carefully guarded, being read only to those who have been initiated into the greatest mysteries."

Mysterious initiations into secret knowledge like the Pythagoreans, and then like the Essenes, a disregard for property and wealth, which should be held in common. But you will remember someone in Rome did not like the *hierophantic instructions of the Lord* so they cut sections out of Mark's Gospel that revealed what Jesus was really about. For example the Lazarus story cut from between verses 34 and 35 of Mark 10:

"And going out of the tomb they came into the house of the youth, for he was rich. And after six days Jesus told him what to do and in the evening the youth comes to him, wearing a linen cloth over his naked body. And he remained with him that night, for Jesus taught him the mystery of the kingdom of God."

The Jewish Talmud also suggests Jesus was teaching a mystic Judaism.

'Jeschu was taken during his boyhood to Egypt, where he was initiated into the secret doctrines of the priests, and on his return to Palestine gave himself up to the practice of magic.'

Mysticism is not alien to the Jewish mind. The Kabbalah is the name applied to the whole range of Jewish mystical activity. Was this type of mysticism what Jesus taught and Lazarus and the Magdalene revealed to the Jews of Gaul? The Encyclopedias state:

'Historically, Kabbalah emerged after earlier forms of Jewish mysticism, in 12th to 13th century Spain and Southern France.'

Right where Lazarus and the Magdalene taught was where the Kabbalah blossomed, on the border between France and Spain. I am not saying they taught the Kabbalah but that they were preaching deeper and more spiritual ideas that could stimulate others.

I would also suggest that these Jews were the rich and wealth-ado families who had escaped the murderous, revolutionary fundamentalism in Israel, so a spiritual philosophy of Judaism may have great appeal.

I should add that according to local legend, Lazarus is teaching in synagogues, a mystic version of Judaism with levels of initiation, while I would imagine the Magdalene does not teach in the Synagogue as this is not allowed and all images of her preaching are in the open air.

So if this is what the Bethany family were teaching in Gaul, one has to ask would Paul, who never knew Jesus, dare to contradict the story told by the people who not only knew Jesus intimately, but appear to be his closest friends. It would certainly take some gall. You would think not but read his letters where he speaks about how God 'chose' him and *'revealed his son in him'*, how the Gospel, as he taught it 'among the gentiles', was the result of a direct *'revelation of Jesus Christ' (Gal. 1:15),* and how if anyone preached a Gospel contrary to the one he had preached – *'even an Angel in Heaven'* – he is to be accursed'.

These astonishing claims show a degree of arrogance that is quite shocking, and of course Paul's sidekick, Luke took up the cudgels and *'accursed the Angel from heaven,* who dared to contradict Paul, that is Mary Magdalene, and assassinated her character any way he could.

On Paul's death in Rome, Luke, takes Mark's Gospel and does his own version of the story, the Gospel of Luke, for gentiles in Rome. He then edits Mark's Gospel and ads the resurrection (to Mark 16:9-20 - an accepted forgery). His teachings are obviously in total contradiction to the teachings of Mary Magdalene in Gaul, so he proceeds to cut very influential members of the Bethany family totally from his Gospel and much of their story from Mark too. He writes the Acts of the Apostles, ignoring the Apostles and mainly tells the story of Paul who claims he is an Apostle because he was the last to see Jesus alive when he was blinded on the road to Damascus. So according to Paul, after the ascension Jesus is supposed to have popped back down to earth, body and soul to convert Paul and make him an Apostle. That means Jesus second coming has already happened so we are actually awaiting his third..

The distinctive traits of Luke's editing are missing when John's Gospel was added to the Bible, and a totally different bias is inserted into John, one that attempts to separate Jesus from the Jews.

The Bethany version of the Jesus story is picked up by the Gnostics who challenge the version coming from Rome. Three hundred years later the Roman Empire officially takes on Paul's religion. So the invented story of Jesus created in Rome has to be repeated, and all semblance of the truth has to be denied. This is the letter from Clement of Alexandria to a cleric called Theodore, praising him for his mendacity.

'You did well in silencing the unspeakable teachings of the Carpocrations. Such men are to be opposed in all ways. For, even if they should say something true, one who loves the truth should not, even so, agree with them. For not all true things are the truth, nor should that truth which merely seems true according to human opinions be preferred to the true truth, that according to the faith.'

Even if they say something true deny it. A tactic that the church have used throughout the ages, although nowadays I notice they try to ridicule it.

What about the Jews in Gaul who have been told by the Magdalene the real story about Jesus, which we are about to reveal, and his ideas of initiation into higher levels of understanding? We know what the church thought about these particular Narbonne Jews from Julian of Toledo's comment about the region, *'a brothel of blaspheming Jews.'* Why are they *blaspheming Jews* as opposed to ordinary Jews? Is it because they believe in Jesus but not the Jesus of the Church, but the Jewish mystical Jesus? So they were clearly *'a brothel of blaspheming Jews'*. They had to be dealt with one way or another and after the Moors were cleared from Spain, the establishment began an assault on this knowledge. This is from the encyclopedia:

'The Inquisition was originally intended primarily to identify heretics among those who converted from Judaism and Islam to Catholicism. The regulation of the faith of newly converted Catholics was intensified after the royal decrees issued in 1492 and 1502 ordering Jews and Muslims to convert to Catholicism or leave Spain. The Inquisition was not definitively abolished until 1834, during the reign of Isabella II.'

Why state that it was specifically to deal with Jews who had converted to Christianity? What form of Christianity had they converted to? Was there developed a new type of Jesus follower that believes in levels of initiation, and the equality of women and the right to discover God through your own gnosis. Were these the Cathars? Academics are unsure of the origin of the Cathars and it could have been part of a general movement against a rich and un-spiritual Church of Rome, but what is clear is that the people of this very region were so predisposed to these ideas that this became the prevalent religion of the exact area that was Septimania. Their Priests are called Perfects! Exactly the term used in Mark's Gospel for those being initiated.

'He arranged a more spiritual gospel for the use of those being perfected.' (Secret Mark)

The Cathars had levels of initiation and women could also become Perfects. The Cathar movement considered the material world as evil and as the Roman Church had become enmeshed in the material world of wealth and power. To the Cathars it was no longer a spiritual movement so they rejected everything to do with the church, its hierarchy, its ceremonies and more to the point, the crucifix itself. They claimed they were the only true Christians and many Knight Templars were Cathars or Cathar sympathizers.

But what did the Roman Church think about these devout followers of Jesus? They launched a bloody crusade against them! The Cathar doctrines struck at the roots of Roman Christianity, the political institutions of Christendom and their literal teachings of the cross and the resurrection. Fear of the spread of these ideas led Pope Innocent III to call a formal crusade and twenty years of war followed against the Cathars and their allies in the Languedoc, in what will later on become known as the Albigensian Crusade. This crusade had a wide support, inspired by a papal decree stating that all land owned by the Cathars and their defenders could be confiscated. Such events made the territory a target for Northern French nobles looking to gain new lands.

"Caediteeos. Novitenim Dominus qui sunteius"—
"Kill them all; God will recognize his own."

After many years and a million slaughtered, the Cathars faded out in the 1270s, and the heresy finally disappeared.

Any doubts that some important information was held by the Jews in this area can be dispelled by the massive attempt to expunge their writings. In an edict dated the 19th of August 1263, King Jayme I of Aragon prescribes that the Jews should either expurgate their own books or have them censored by the Jewish apostate Paulus of Burgos. Failure to obey the command would entail the destruction of the books and a heavy fine.

And it continued, as it is reported by Academic Robert Eisler that in the age of the printing press:

'...the office of censorship was performed by baptized Jews, who were authorized to search private and synagogue libraries for 'blasphemous' i.e. anti Christian literature, and to expurgate it.' (Robert Eisler)

In fact there is a whole chapter in the Jewish Encyclopedia on this type of censorship.

The Hebrew books were demanded from their Jewish possessors in the name of the Inquisition, and were handed over to the local office. Concealment of books was rigorously punished, not only by seizure of the books and by large fines, but, under certain circumstances, also by imprisonment and by confiscation of property. The books collected were examined by the appointed revisers, who destroyed the interdicted ones, and punished their possessors. The objectionable books were then expurgated and restored to their owners with a certificate of censorship. The Jews had to provide the costs of the censorship; that is, the payment of the revisers. It was forbidden, on pain of heavy punishment, to restore the expurgated words, or to supply the missing passages between the lines or in the margins.'

It is interesting that after the book had been censored a signed certificate was added by the censor.

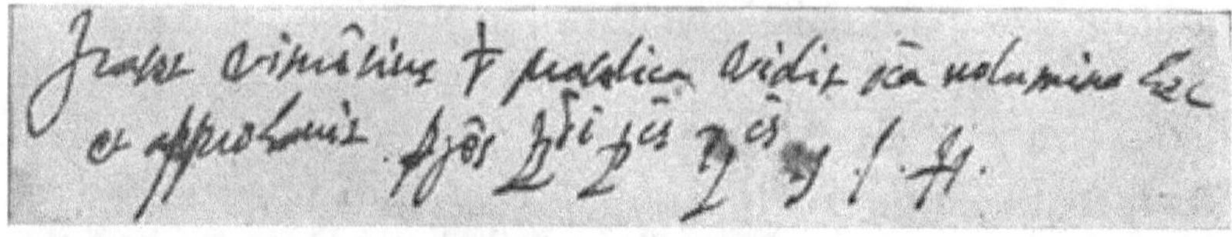

In 1559 the first Papal index of prohibited books appeared which obviously included the Talmud with all its compendiums, glosses, notes, interpretations, and expositions. Luckily a couple of key sections in the Talmud survived.

So now it is time to reveal what Mary Magdalene knew, the true story of Jesus, that may shock you but was certainly known in this area of Gaul up to recent times because there are plenty of heretical images that tell this story in the Magdalene church in Rennes-le-Château.

Chapter Eleven

CONFESSIONS
The first clues

As I have made clear already, the encyclopedias have a number of confused statements about the Templar's formation. The same is true of their demise. This is from the history book I quoted from before.

'The knights were brutally tortured until they confessed to false charges, which included heresy, homosexuality, financial corruption, devil-worshipping, fraud and spitting on the cross.'

This is similarly repeated in the Encyclopedia Britannica:

'King Philip accused the Templars of heresy and immorality; specific charges against them included idol worship (of a bearded male head said to have great powers), worship of a cat, homosexuality, and numerous other errors of belief and practice. At the order's secret initiation rite, it was claimed, the new member denied Christ three times, spat on the crucifix, and was kissed on the base of the spine, on the navel, and on the mouth by the knight presiding over the ceremony. The charges, now recognized to be without foundation.'

So one says they were *'false charges'*, the other, that the charges were *without foundation*, and this is repeated by the church even today. How do they know these were false charges? What do they mean the charges were *without foundation?* Are they saying these things did not happen at secret initiations? Surely only a Templar can tell you if they were false or real, and under torture they did confess to them. But surely only under torture would they admit to these accusations because, we know from the rituals of Freemasons, a novitiate swears that if he divulges any of the secrets his tongue will be pulled out and several other awful things will happen to him. So your choices in this situation are limited to, tongue being removed and killed in a variety of nasty ways for giving out secret information, or burning at the stake for spitting on the cross.

The fact is, they did spit on the cross and the most ludicrous suggestion by some is that they were practicing in case they were captured by Moslems!

But here is a more reasoned approach.

'Of all charges leveled against the Templars, the most serious were those of blasphemy and heresy – of denying, trampling and spitting on the cross. It is not clear what precisely this alleged ritual was intended to signify – what, in other words, the Templars were actually repudiating. Were they repudiating Christ? Or were they simply repudiating the crucifixion? And whatever they repudiated, what exactly did they extol in its stead? No one has satisfactorily answered those question.'(H.B.H.G. Baigent, Leigh & Lincoln)

I think you will know the answer to that question before you have finished reading this book.

In Freemasonry the higher degrees are denied by United Grand Lodge; but of the 33 degrees the 27th Degree of *'the Grand Commander of the Temple'* is of interest to us. It is a chivalric degree where the members sit at a round table to interrogate the candidate. The ritual tells of the *false* condemnation of the Knights Templar and the importance of the *denial of the cross.*

But how can it be both claiming, a false condemnation of the Templars, and at the same time repeating what they were condemned for, denial of the cross? Were the accusations false or true? Did they or didn't they deny the cross? If they denied the cross then the accusations were not false! They were true. How can we unravel this?

It certainly looks like the Knights Templar did deny the cross and they have left that belief alive in esoteric groups in France even to present day. Look at this from Grand Master, Claude Debussy who wrote this in a review, *"Perhaps it's to destroy that scandalous legend that Jesus Christ died on the cross.'*

Other heretical groups were also accused of denying Jesus died on the cross, some even saying that a substitute took his place. That is the belief of the Muslims too who were not under the influence of the Holy Roman Empire. They state in their works that Pilate did not crucify Jesus but he was substituted.

Furthermore Canon Alfred Lilley, a well known British academic, clergyman, on returning from Paris where he had been studying and translating documents at the Seminary of St. Sulpice, told his friend, the Rev. Bartlett that he had incontrovertible proof that the crucifixion was a fraud and that Jesus was alive, well after the date of the supposed crucifixion. Lilley believed the document he had seen was authentic and had been in the possession of the Cathars during the 12th Century even though they it was much older. These were not minor conspiratorial figures, Lilley had been Canon and Chancellor of Hereford Cathedral and Rev Bartlett had a Masters Degree from Oxford as well as a

Medical degree and was a member of the Royal College of Surgeons. So if these high powered members of the church were suggesting that there existed a document that claimed the crucifixion was a hoax then it must be taken seriously.

So is this why the Templars denied the cross and even spat on it? Can there be any validity in this denial since nearly all Academics, Atheist or Christian, accept that, if Jesus existed, he was, without question crucified by Pontius Pilate? But why is this not questioned when heretics were being burnt at the stake rather than retract their belief. There is only one direction for us to go and that is to investigate every aspect of the crucifixion using all sources, including esoteric groups, to discover the facts behind the real story of Jesus and Pilate.

Chapter Twelve

PONTIUS PILATE AND JESUS

It has been stated for centuries that Pilate crucified Jesus in 32 AD. Why? The date is absolutely impossible because, by comparing events in the Gospels with known events in Rome a very revealing timeline unfolds. This is because there is a direct relationship between the death of John the Baptist and the date of the death of the Emperor Tiberius.

Tiberius came to power in the year 14 AD and died in March 37 AD. Towards the end of his reign in the year 32 or 33, it is alleged by the Church and accepted by most academics, that Pontius Pilate crucified Jesus. Luke's Gospel offers us another useful date.

'In the fifteenth year of the reign of Tiberius Caesar, when Pontius Pilate was governor of Judea, Herod tetrarch of Galilee, his brother Philip tetrarch of Iturea... the word of God came to John son of Zechariah in the wilderness. He went into all the country around the Jordan, preaching a baptism of repentance.' (Luke 3:1)

From this one can calculate that John the Baptist came preaching 15 years after Tiberius began his reign, which gives us the year AD 29. It also offers us the names of two of the sons of Herod the Great, Philip and Herod. Philip was married to Herodias, who later married this same brother Herod and the Bible tells how:

'Herod had arrested John the Baptist and bound him and put him in prison because of Herodias, his brother Philip's

wife, for John had been saying to him: "It is not lawful for you to have her." Herod wanted to kill John, but he was afraid of the people, because they considered John a prophet. On Herod's birthday the daughter of Herodias danced for the guests and pleased Herod so much that he promised on oath to give her whatever she asked. Prompted by her mother, she said, "Give me here on a platter the head of John the Baptist." The king was distressed, but because of his oaths, he ordered that her request be granted and had John beheaded in the prison. His head was brought in on a platter and given to the girl, who carried it to her mother. John's disciples came and took his body and buried it. Then they went and told Jesus.' (Matthew 14:1)

At no time in the Gospels are we given the name of the dance, which has now become so famous. But we do learn the name of Herodias' daughter, from, Josephus who was actually writing a few years after these events. In one of his books we find out that Herodias daughter was called Salome.

It is after the death of John the Baptist that Jesus begins his ministry by addressing the multitude. Just two to three years later, according to accepted belief, Jesus is arrested and then crucified by Pontius Pilate. If one puts all these events together the first thing that must strike you is the short time John was baptizing in the desert; surely too short a time to have become so famous.

29 – John starts baptizing
29 – John baptizes Jesus
30 – John is arrested
30 – John is beheaded
30 – Jesus begins his mission
32/33 – Jesus is crucified.

If you find these dates unlikely, it actually becomes impossible if you read these same events in the works of Josephus. Although his two books have been heavily edited by Christians so as not to contradict the Bible, they contain information that has slipped through because of its convoluted nature. Here we will unravel one such event, the death of John the Baptist, by cross-referencing known Roman history with Josephus' writings. It is complex but stick with me, as we follow Josephus' description of the death of John the Baptist.

Firstly he describes the death of Philip in 34 AD! Then he tells us that to marry Philip's wife, Herod divorced his first wife, who was the daughter of King Aretas of Petra. Herod then married Herodias as is mentioned in the Bible. But what is not in the Bible is the fact that King Aretas' daughter went home crying to her father, who raised an army and attacked Israel. Herod sent his army into battle but they were completely wiped out. Distraught, Herod complained to the Emperor Tiberius, who sent a message to the legate of Syria, Vitellius, to either capture King Aretas and bring him to Rome or bring his head. Vitellius set out, but before he could attack, news came that Tiberius had died and he retreated to await instruction from the new Emperor, Caligula. Josephus also gives us the information that when this same Vitellius arrived in Syria in 36 AD he sacked Pontius Pilate.

These events described by Josephus, are almost impossible to fit into the Biblical timeline as presented above.

29 John the Baptist starts baptizing.

34 Philip dies.

35 Herod divorces first wife and marries Herodias.

35 John the Baptist complains about this marriage.

35/36 John the Baptist is arrested and beheaded.

36 Vitellius becomes Legate of Syria and fires Pilate.

36 King Aretas destroys Herod's army.

37 Tiberius orders Vitellius into battle.

37 (March) Tiberius dies.

37 (April) Vitellius stops attack after news from Rome.

37 Jesus dies?

Given that Jesus' mission was for two years after the Baptist death in 35 AD, this scenario has Jesus alive till at least 37 AD! The only way to solve the problem is to advance the divorce of Herod and his marriage to Herodias to before Philip dies and before John began baptizing in 29 AD. That of course has the problem that King Aretas attacks Herod eight years after the rejection of his daughter, which is surely too long a time before taking revenge. But in a later paragraph in Josephus we do have an attempt to create just such a possibility.

'Herodias took it upon herself to confound the laws of our country, and divorced herself from her husband while he was alive, and was married to Herod, her husband's brother.' (Josephus Antiquities.)

So although chronologically Josephus writes, firstly of Philip's death in 34 AD, followed by Herod's divorce, this later addition clearly states the divorce was before Philip died, so the date could be anywhere from 28 to 34.

As mentioned, if the divorce was in 28 AD, then this makes King Areta's revenge attack, happen eight to nine years after the insult, which does appear unlikely. Furthermore, I would suggest that *'divorced her husband while he was alive'* looks very much like an insertion because you cannot divorce your husband if he is dead.

Have you ever heard anyone say Elizabeth Taylor divorced Richard Burton while he was alive? Of course not, it is ridiculous. So this emphasis on 'alive' seems to be because it had been noticed that if Philip had died before Herodias took up with Herod then the Baptist would still be alive after 34 AD and so Jesus could not be crucified in 32 or 33 AD. This laughable insertion *'divorced her husband while he was alive'* almost suggests the opposite is true, and even presents us with the clear possibility that the authorities knew very well that Josephus was right when he placed Philips death before the marriage, and had blatantly tried to change the facts.

Perhaps you believe, that it was just Josephus' bad structuring, putting Philip's death before Herodias marriage to Herod, but there is more evidence to consider. Just look how Josephus begins the second paragraph after he reports Philip's death:

'Now some of the Jews thought that the destruction of Herod's army came from God as a just punishment of what Herod had done against John, who was called the Baptist. For Herod had killed this good man...'(Joseph 'Antiq')

Now if the Baptist had been killed nine years before the destruction of Herod's army, surely nobody would link the two events. The destruction of the army in or around 36 AD must have been no more than six months to a year after the Baptist's death, for them to be linked, which again places the death around 35 AD, three to four years after the supposed date of Jesus' crucifixion.

Also consider this: I have been quoting from Josephus' *'The Antiquity of the Jews'* book, which was written around the year 93 AD and describes the whole history of the Jews since Abraham migrated from Mesopotamia. But his first book, '*The Jewish War*' written around 75 AD covers just the hundred-year period that leads to the War which Josephus participated in. Now clearly the 'Antiquities' book can only mention Philip's death and the Baptist's arrest in passing but the 'War' book will obviously cover them more fully. So if we turn to the 'War' book and see what it says about the death of Philip, the divorce of Herod's first wife, the marriage to Herodias and the total destruction of Herod's army, we get this:

NOTHING! Not a word about any of it. No destruction of Herod's army, no John the Baptist and not even a mention of the important Legate of Syria, Vitellius in the whole book. Did he forget this most important person who sacked Pilate and played a major part in bringing a degree of peace to Israel (and whose son became Emperor). Surely that is not credible nor is the absence of the total destruction of Herod's army, who must have policed Galilee for the Romans. If omission can be classed as evidence, we have the most telling evidence ever that these events had to be cut because they contradicted the Gospel story, by giving us a more detailed and telling account of the Baptist's death than the 'Antiquities' book does.

But it does not end there. All our earliest versions of Josephus' books come from copies made by Christian monks, around the eleventh century. There is though one version discovered in Russia in 1886, which is a translation from the original Greek into Old Russian. And if the Baptist was cut from our version of the 'War' book, guess what; he is still in the Slavonic version. And after Philip dies comes this:

'And Herod, his brother, took his wife Herodias. And because of her all the doctors of the Law abhorred him, but durst not

accuse him before his face. But only that one, whom they called a wild man, came to him in anger and spake: "Why hast thou taken the wife of thy brother? As thy brother hath died a death void of pity, thou too wilt be reaped off by the heavenly sickle…. Now when Herod heard [this], he was filled with wrath and commanded that they should beat him and drive him away. But he accused Herod incessantly wherever he found him, and right up to the time when Herod put him under arrest and gave orders to slay him.' (Slavonic Josephus)

So clearly the marriage between Herod and Herodias is after Philip's death. And this statement by the Baptist, *'thy brother hath died a death void of pity'* clearly makes the Baptist alive after the death of Philip in 34. Furthermore, if we take the word 'incessantly' at face value, we have the Baptist giving Herod a hard time for several years, or at least quite a bit after Phillip's death. Even after Herod decides to deal with John, in all versions of the story, he does not kill him right away but imprisons him.

So I think we can be pretty sure that John the Baptist was alive and kicking well past the supposed date of Jesus' crucifixion in 32 AD. All we need to do now is prove the Bible is correct, and that Jesus did not start his ministry till after the Baptist's death, in 35.

'King Herod heard about this, for Jesus' name had become well known. Some were saying, 'John the Baptist has been raised from the dead, and that is why miraculous powers are at work in him….' But when Herod heard this, he said, 'John, whom I beheaded, has been raised from the dead!' (Mk 6:14)

So Herod thinks Jesus is the resurrected John, which clearly makes Jesus alive after the Baptist's death. There are many other quotes that say the same, one even by Jesus himself:

"From the days of John the Baptist until now, the kingdom of heaven has been subjected to violence." (Mat 11:12)

Here Jesus is clearly talking about a person who has died some time ago. But why was the kingdom of heaven subjected to violence? That is something we will confront later.

So, if Jesus preached for a couple of years after the death of John, it would take us to around 38 AD, well after the date Pontius Pilate left Judea. This creates a new timeline where many of my dates are confirmed, while others can only be out by, at the most, six months to a year.

34 AD Philip dies. [confirmed]
34 AD Herod divorces his first wife. [confirmed]
        She returns to her father, King Aretas. [confirmed]
34/35 AD Herod marries Herodias.
34/35 AD The Baptist complains about the marriage.
34/35 AD Herod arrests the Baptist.
35 AD Lucius Vitellius becomes legate of Syria.
        [confirmed]
A35 AD Herod kills the Baptist.
        (Could be before the above)
35/36 AD Aretas goes to war and wins. [confirmed]
        (Now within a year of the divorce)
35/36 AD Vitellius sacks Pontius Pilate. [confirmed]
37 AD Tiberius dies (March) [confirmed]
37 AD Vitellius goes to arrest King Aretas but stops when
        news of Tiberius arrives. [confirmed]
37 AD Vitellius arrives back in Jerusalem to be welcomed
        by cheering crowds. He then cancels certain taxes
        and allows the Judean Priests custody over their
        own vestments. [confirmed]
37-38 AD In this period of peace created by Vitellius, Jesus

preaches and performs miraculous cures.
38 AD Jesus dies?

Could this date of 38 AD for Jesus' death be true? If you read old texts carefully every now and then some truth slips through the Christian censors. In this case they missed editing a statement by church father, Epiphanius who wrote that Jesus brother, James died in 62 AD after having been head of the church for twenty-four years. It looks an innocent enough statement in itself, which is why it has slipped through the editing process. But take twenty-four from sixty-two and it gives you the key date of 38 AD. It is accepted that, James took over the leadership after Jesus' death, but now it appears that that date is 38 AD.

It seems so obvious that I tried to find academics who have unraveled this before me. I finally discovered Dr. Robert Eisler who died in 1945 and could translate from original documents as he could read Aramaic, ancient Greek, Hebrew, and Latin. Eisler became famous for sifting through all the various versions of Josephus, in all the different languages and thereby piecing together a picture of what Jesus must have been like. He also was an expert on the Josippon, which is a shortened re-write of Josephus but it has been translated in many forms, which are not so standardized by Christians. Eisler kept finding edited sections that imply the date of 38 AD. This one relates to a version of Josephus in the Bibliotheque Nationale (MS Hebr.1280 written by Juda b. Shelomo)

The archetype of this redaction no longer contained anything about the crucifixion under Pilate, and the copyist thus had to mention it in a different context, notwithstanding the risk of creating a false impression, to the effect that Jesus had been executed in the reign of Caligula.

Caligula ruled from 37 AD to 41 AD. You can see Eisler thinks this is a mistake of the copyist but of course it is exactly as I am presenting the case, that Jesus died in 38 AD.

My timeline virtually confirms that Pontius Pilate had nothing at all to do with the death of Jesus. But it does not tell us whether Jesus was or was not crucified, but it certainly contradicts the accepted story. It also makes the date 32 AD pretty impossible. Why not a more likely date like 36 AD while Pilate was still in Judea? Did something happen in 32 AD that this date has been presented to us over the centuries as the date of the crucifixion?

An academic who does suggest 36 AD is Prof. Robert Eisenman. But even though at one point he writes:

"For Epiphanius , James reigned in Jerusalem for twenty-four years after the Assumption of Jesus, which if Josephus is correct, would place Jesus crucifixion in 38 CE." (Eisenman- 'James the Brother of Jesus')

He obviously cannot quite believe his own calculations as he firstly agrees with me:

"Josephus' reference to John the Baptist is perhaps the most complete...one of the things the notice clears up is the year of John's death, approximately 35-36 CE, which is, of course, totally at odds with how it is presented in the Gospels."

But then sadly follows this with:

"If John died in 35-36 CE that means that Jesus must have died later in 36 CE."

Why 36? Surely Jesus' mission was not just for a couple of months after John's death? Why have those who have accepted my reasoning, and even noted the date of 38 AD concluded that Jesus death was so soon after John's death?

Clearly after realizing the impossibility of a date of 32 or 33, they have gone to the latest date Pontius Pilate was in Judea, 36 AD. They clearly cannot accept the idea that Pontius Pilate was not involved in the death of Jesus. This is because there is a clear statement by the Roman writer Tacitus in his book *'Annals of Rome'*, that Jesus was crucified by Pilate.

'Nero fastened the guilt and inflicted the most exquisite tortures on a class hated for their abominations, called Christians by the populace. Christus, from whom the name had its origin, suffered the extreme penalty during the reign of Tiberius at the hands of one of our procurators, Pontius Pilatus, and a most mischievous superstition, thus checked for the moment.' (Tacitus)

No Christian would describe their religion, as a *'mischievous superstition'* so one has to accept this is not a Christian forgery but Tacitus' actual words. So I am going to have to prove that at the same time as accepting Tacitus statement I have to show he does not actually contradict my timeline that shows Pilate had absolutely nothing to do with the death of Jesus. A position, which I am sure you think, is not only indefensible, but ludicrous. How can I accept Tacitus and then say, Jesus was not crucified by Pilate? So I am going to have to confront your justified skepticism and that of the Academic world.

Chapter Thirteen

THE CRUCIFIXION?

Before I bring more evidence that Pilate was not involved with Jesus, I need to give a little background information about the Crucifixion of Jesus. The most astonishing thing is that there are no paintings or sculptures of Jesus on the cross! Okay, you have seen millions of such paintings, but there are none from the first hundred years after his death, and none from the second hundred years, and none from the third hundred years after his death. It is not until the fifth century that scenes of the Crucifixion began to appear. And this is the very first, which appears on a single small relief panel in the top left corner of a wooden door of the Church of Santa Sabina in Rome.

Yes, this is it, the very first image of the Crucifixion of Jesus. And this Crucifixion panel is one of twenty-four, high on the left hand, side door, a rather out-of-the-way location for the central tenet of Christianity.

Santa Sabina was consecrated in AD 440, almost exactly 400 years after the event. Can you believe there is no image of Jesus being crucified before this one, in any church anywhere? And even this one is a bit weird; the crosses are not clearly represented, only two vertical posts seemingly dividing the composition into sections. It is also puzzling that the crucified figures are not attached to crosses.

But, not only were there no images of Jesus on the cross but the vertical cross was not even used by Christians as their primary image. When excavating a Roman villa in England I remember seeing on TV the archaeologists announcing that the occupants were Christian, because they uncovered an X cross in a mosaic floor. This then was the original cross symbol used by Christians; not the vertical cross at all but the X shaped cross of the Chi-rho.

This appears in pagan papyri, where the sign was used for the Greek word 'chreston', meaning auspicious. It was only after the time of the Emperor Constantine, who converted the Roman Empire to Christianity, that the vertical cross began to be seen as the new symbol for Christianity. We know the vertical cross was not in use when Constantine fought the Battle of Milvian bridge in 312, even though in paintings and films, Constantine is shown seeing a cross in the sky, which stimulated him to paint it on the shields of his soldiers, which brought him victory.

But we have contemporary evidence written by the Christian, Lactantius, who was both a friend of Constantine and tutor to his son, Crispus that it was not that cross.

'Constantine was advised in his sleep to mark the heavenly sign of God on the shields and then engage in battle. He did as he was commanded and by means of a slanted letter X with the top of its head bent round he marked Christ on the shields. Armed with this sign the army took up its weapons... The army of Maxentius was seized with terror and he himself fled to the bridge where he was hurled into the Tiber. (Lactantius De Mort)

So clearly these paintings are wrong and we can be reasonably certain that the X was changed to the vertical cross only after the time of Constantine when the Roman Empire took over the Christian religion around 330 AD.

From this you might expect me to conclude that Jesus was never crucified, thereby supporting the Templar's *'denial of the cross,'* but I am not. I am only going to repeat what the Gnostics said, that the crucifixion must not be taken literally. This clearly is very confusing as you are either crucified or you are not. But there is an explanation to the beliefs of the Gnostics, who were followers of Jesus in the neighboring countries of Israel, Egypt and Syria. These followers of Jesus certainly came into conflict with the Christian Church several thousand miles away in Rome.

Before we unravel the whole story to reveal the reasons behind the Templar's beliefs and the vicious attacks on the Magdalene, let me invite you to read again the letter sent by Louis Fouquet after a meeting in Rome with the mysterious painter Poussin.

'He and I discussed certain things, which I shall with ease be able to explain to you in detail – things which will give you, through Monsieur Poussin, advantages which even kings would have great pains to draw from him, and which, according to him, it is possible that nobody else will ever rediscover in the centuries to come.' (Letter: Louis Fouquet)

Remember Fouquet was arrested and was kept completely incommunicado, it is said even the jailers were not allowed to communicate with him, and all his correspondence was confiscated and sent directly to King Louis XIV.

Now, in the next five chapters I am going to reveal to you the information that Poussin possessed which he thought, *'...that nobody else will ever rediscover in the centuries to come.'*

The century has come!

Chapter Fourteen

THE FIRST CONTRADICTION
Galilee

We do not know what documents Canon Alfred Lilley had seen that convinced him Pilate did not crucify Jesus but actually we don't need them because there are two totally different stories running parallel in the Gospels. One has been emphasized, so you know it well, and the other is ignored. I would say that it is reasonably easy to spot which side of the two stories is true and which is an interpolation; that is, once you know what the purpose of the insertion is. The first of these contradictions happens right at the beginning of Jesus ministry when he finds his first disciples.

'As Jesus walked beside the Sea of Galilee, he saw Simon and his brother Andrew casting a net into the lake, for they were fishermen. Jesus said, "Come, follow me,"(Mark 1:16)

And just like that they follow him. A lovely story we all marvel at. And many academic papers have been written about the Sea of Galilee fishermen, the type of boats they used, etc, etc. I should add that an official part of the regalia worn by the Pope as head of the Catholic Church and successor to Peter is the Fisherman's Ring. So you might believe there is absolutely no question, Simon Peter and his brother are fishermen who suddenly drop their nets and follow Jesus. So you may be surprised that a totally different story of the finding of these very same disciples, Andrew and Simon Peter is in the Gospels!

*'The next day John the Baptist saw Jesus and said to two
disciples, "Look, the Lamb of God!"
When the two disciples heard him say this, they followed
Jesus. Turning around, Jesus saw them following and asked,
"What do you want?"
They said, "Rabbi, where are you staying?"
"Come," he replied, "and you will see."
So they went and saw where he was staying, and they spent
that day with him. It was about four in the afternoon.
Andrew, Simon Peter's brother, was one of the two who heard
what John had said and who had followed Jesus. The first
thing Andrew did was to find his brother Simon and tell him,
"We have found the Messiah." And he brought him to Jesus.'
(John 1:40)*

Suddenly they are not the romantic fishermen at all, they
are just boring followers of John the Baptist who spend
some time with Jesus before deciding to become his
disciples. And the event is not happening in Galilee but
Judea, by the river Jordon about eighteen miles from
Jerusalem.

Furthermore it says, Andrew immediately goes to find
his brother Simon Peter who is living somewhere in Judea,
not by the Sea of Galilee at all.

But even more to the point, in 'Acts of the Apostles',
Simon Peter is actually reported as saying:

*'Now I, and those with me, can witness to everything he did
throughout the countryside of Judea and in Jerusalem itself.'
(Acts 10:39)*

So they are witnesses to everything he did in Judea but they
are not witnesses to anything going on in Galilee. In fact,
scholars have noticed that all the passages that mention

Galilee are later additions, which are oddly incorrect. For instance, Mark says that Jesus went through Sidon on his way from Tyre to the Sea of Galilee. Problem is Sidon is in the opposite direction and there was no road anyway in the first century. And Mark writes:

*'And passing **along by the Sea of Galilee** he saw Simon and Andrew.' (Mark 1:16)*

In Greek the verb *passing along* is not used with the preposition *by*. So if one removed the bold part of this sentence you will have the correct syntax.

'And passing he saw Simon and Andrew.' (Mark 1:16)

Furthermore in Mark 5 there is a story where Gerasa slopes down to the Sea of Galilee, but Gerasa (modern Jerash) is thirty miles away from the sea.

I have to wonder if this is Luke's handiwork again because I get the feeling that Luke had never been to Israel? And Biblical expert, Professor Robert Eisenman, writes:

'A great deal of trouble is taken by these writers to get Jesus to Galilee.'(Robert Eisenman: Jesus and the Dead Sea Scrolls)

Eisenman has no idea why; he is just stating a fact as he sees it with no particular conclusion. However I will be explaining why these interpolations were important to church authorities.

Now I said it is easy to spot the real from the invented and although John's version of recruiting the disciples is less remarkable, it does seem the more likely, so why do the synoptic Gospels move all this to the Sea of Galilee and make these same disciples, fishermen who leave their employ on a silly whim? In fact John's Gospel places most of the Jesus story in Jerusalem.

'Now there is in Jerusalem near the Sheep Gate a pool, which in Aramaic is called Bethesda and which is surrounded by five covered colonnades. Here a great number of disabled people used to lie.' (John 5:2)

By this pool, Jesus famously tells the lame man to pick up his mat and walk. Then on another day (John 9:7) he cures a blind man by the pool of Siloam. And in wintertime we get this:

'At that time the Feast of Dedication took place at Jerusalem. It was winter, and Jesus was walking in the temple, in the colonnade of Solomon. (John 10:22)'

So Jesus is in and out of Jerusalem all the time not just at the end of his ministry.

John even contradicts the other Gospels about the overturning of the moneylenders outside the Temple. He places it right at the beginning of Jesus' ministry, while the synoptic Gospels delay the event till they have Jesus arrive in Jerusalem at the end. This contradiction could well be the reason they are making a big deal of his grand entry into Jerusalem on Palm Sunday, riding on the donkey, but then ignore the fact that he does this same journey at least four more times that week with no such fuss. Also a week before Palm Sunday we have the raising of Lazarus in Bethany, just a mile and a half from Jerusalem, which makes it hard to imagine that he did not go to visit the Temple then.

We have many references to Jesus' brother, James, in the works of the early church fathers and they all talk about James being in Jerusalem and spending a lot of time in the Temple, which suggests that Jesus was there or thereabouts too. And so it seems, because we have seen that Jesus appears to have his base two miles from Jerusalem in Bethany, where he and his disciples often go overnight. The evidence seems to point to the fact that Jesus spent most of his time in Judea not Galilee and even the name Jesus of Nazareth appears to be part of this process of deception.

It is easy to show that Jesus never lived in Nazareth, as he was never originally called Jesus of Nazareth. Firstly, we have very little evidence that Nazareth, as a village, existed at the time; if it did then it was a very small village. So why was this insignificant appellation added to Jesus' name. Thomas of York makes sense, as York is a well-known town; or Alfred of Wessex after a known region, but Erik of Ecclesfield makes no sense whatsoever, as nobody but the people of Ecclesfield (apologies to the villagers North of Sheffield) would have any idea what the hell we are talking about. So Jesus of Nazareth is not only very unlikely, it is silly! Jesus of Sepphoris is more likely, after the major town three miles from Nazareth; or Jesus the Galilean after the region. Unfortunately, we already have the important rebel, Judas the Galilean functioning at the time so two Galileans at the same time would be a bit weird.

There is a document, alleged to have been written by a Roman official, Publius Lentulus, in Jerusalem during Jesus lifetime. You will probably see it is a flattering forgery but it has some interesting points:

'There has appeared in our city a man of great power named Jesus. The people call him a prophet and his disciples the Son of God. He is in stature a man of middle height and well proportioned, with a venerable face. His hair is the color of ripe chestnuts smooth almost to the ears, but above them wavy and curly with a slight bluish radiancy. And it flows

over his shoulders. It is parted in the middle after the fashion of the people of Nazareth.'

Okay, the usual flattering description of Jesus except for one point, his hair is parted in the middle after the *'fashion of the people of Nazareth'*. What a crazy and extremely unlikely idea! I'm sure the nine or ten adult males of this village of Nazareth did not have a particularly distinctive well-known hairstyle. The Bible does give us this:

'Having been warned in a dream, he <u>withdrew to the district of Galilee</u>, and he went and lived in a town called Nazareth. So was fulfilled what was said through the prophets: 'He will be called a Nazarene.'' (Matthew 2:23)

There actually is no prophesy in the Old Testament that says *he will be called a Nazarene*? The word only appears in the New Testament. But Nazarene must have some meaning other than a person, with a particular hairstyle, from a probably non-existent village in Galilee. The Old Testament tells us:

'The Lord said to Moses, "If a man or woman wants to make a vow of separation to the Lord as a Nazirite, he must not eat anything that comes from the grapevine. During the entire period of his vow of separation no razor may be used on his head; he must let the hair of his head grow long." (Numbers 6:5)

A Nazirite then is someone dedicated to God. Samson for instance says to Delilah:

"No razor has ever been used on my head," said Samson, "because I have been a Nazirite set apart to God since birth. If my head were shaved, my strength would leave me." (Judges 16:17)

If Jesus was not dedicated to God; not a Nazirite; it would be a bit of a surprise and the very earliest images of Jesus show him with long hair, often parted in the middle, a distinct feature of a Nazarene; not a villager from Nazareth! So Nazarenes are a group of people, a movement, perhaps started by Jesus or that Jesus belonged to because Paul is found guilty of being one:

"We have found this man to be a troublemaker, stirring up riots among the Jews all over the world. He is a ringleader of the Nazarene sect." (Acts 24:5)

Changing Jesus the Nazarene to Jesus of Nazareth appears to be part of the same attempt to link Jesus with Galilee. But what possible reason could there be for this desperate attempt to place Jesus in Galilee? It clearly was extremely important to someone for all the machinations that have been shown. I will repeat again Professor Robert Eisenman's comment:

'A great deal of trouble is taken by these writers to get Jesus to Galilee.'(Robert Eisenman: Jesus and the Dead Sea Scrolls)

Eisenman is just stating a fact as he sees it, with no particular conclusion. He is mystified by the trouble the writer, or writers in the synoptic Gospels have taken to place Jesus in Galilee. But the most extraordinary thing is that when you solve the mystery of Galilee, the whole story of Jesus' crucifixion unravels and suggests the Knights Templar had every cause to deny the cross.

Chapter Fifteen

THE SECOND CONTRADICTION
Stoning

After the arrest, Jesus is brought before the Jewish Sanhedrin.

'Again the high priest was questioning him, "Are You the Christ, the Son of the Blessed One?" And Jesus said, "I am…" "You have heard the blasphemy; how does it seem to you?" And they all condemned him to be deserving of death. (Mark 14:61)

They find Jesus guilty of blasphemy and condemn him to death, but then they take him to Pilate who suggests:

"Take him and judge him by your own law, said Pilate" "But we have no right to execute anyone," they objected.' (John 18:30)

Are the Sanhedrin allowed to stone people or not? If there was such a rule it must have been introduced by the Romans so how come Pilate does not know about it?

Pilate said, "Take him and judge him by your own law."

So John's Gospel, and only John's, has this one statement that the Sanhedrin are not allowed to stone Jews for blasphemy. But there is a totally different story in the Bible, which appears straight after in Acts of the Apostles.

'The elders dragged Stephen away and brought him before the Council. "We have heard this man say that the Nazarene, Jesus, will destroy this place and alter the customs which Moses handed down to us." (Acts 6:13)

Stephen then makes a long speech on how all the Prophets were persecuted by the establishment, which riles the members of the Sanhedrin.

'They cried out with a loud voice, and covered their ears and rushed at him with one impulse. When they had driven him out of the city, they began stoning him. They went on stoning Stephen as he called on the Lord and said, "Lord Jesus, receive my spirit!" Then falling on his knees, he fell asleep.' (Acts 7)

So they can stone people for blasphemy. Was the speech in John's Gospel that the Sanhedrin are not allowed to kill people an insertion because there is even more evidence:

'Then after this he said to the disciples, "Let us go to Judea again." The disciples said to him, "Rabbi, the Jews were just now seeking to stone you, and are you going there again?" (John 11:7)

I would also remind you that Jesus saves a prostitute from being stoned by announcing to the crowd, "Let he who has not sinned throw the first stone." And another time Jesus is nearly stoned himself:

The Jews picked up stones again to stone him. Jesus answered them, "I have shown you many good works from the Father; for which of them are you going to stone me?" The Jews answered him, "It is not for a good work that we are going to stone you but for blasphemy, because you, being a man, make yourself God." (John 10:31)

I should also remind you that after the raising of Lazarus we get this:

'A large crowd came, not only to see Jesus, but also to see Lazarus, whom he had raised from the dead. So the chief priests made plans to kill Lazarus as well.' (John12: 9)

Don't the Chief Priests know they are not allowed to kill people? Certainly Josephus, writing at the time, says the Priests can stone people.

'The Priests who were ordained to be the inspectors of all, and the judges in doubtful cases, and the punishers of those that were condemned. (Josephus 'Against Apion')

And this is followed by instruction on the law of marriage:

'A husband is allowed only to sleep with his wife, but to have to do with another man's wife, is a wicked thing and punishable by death.'

And then a list of other sins that are punishable by death, but not a word here that the Roman's have put an end to this process. I would add that it appears that not only are the Sanhedrin allowed to stone people to death but the Jewish King, Herod Antipas, has just chopped off John the Baptists head for questioning his legitimacy, so he too has the right to kill, especially someone usurping his title and claiming he is the rightful 'King of the Jews.'

I hope we can at least agree that one minute the Sanhedrin are not allowed to stone people for blasphemy, the next minute they are doing just that by stoning Stephen. There is clearly something very strange going on, because without this one statement in John's Gospel, the whole process of taking Jesus to a reluctant Pontius Pilate makes no sense whatsoever.

THE STONING FROM THE MOVIE 'LIFE OF BRIAN'
WHERE WOMEN WEAR BEARDS TO ATTEND AN EVENT
THAT HAS SUPPOSEDLY BEEN BANNED BY THE ROMANS.
WHO IS RIGHT, THE BIBLE OR THE MONTY PYTHONS?

Chapter Sixteen

THE THIRD CONTRADICTION
Arrest

In the Gospels there are again two different stories of the arrest of Jesus. Firstly the synoptic Gospels have him arrested by a crowd with temple guards.

'Just as He was speaking, Judas, one of the Twelve, appeared with a crowd armed with swords and clubs, sent from the chief priests, the teachers of the law, and the elders.'

So this is a Jewish event with a crowd sent by the Chief Priests. But John has a totally different story.

'So the Roman cohort and the commander and the officers of the Jews, arrested Jesus and bound him.'

There are no Roman soldiers in the synoptics but in John there is a 'cohort' of soldiers. A cohort is a battalion of around 800 soldiers and four centurions. In fact Josephus states that normally there is only one cohort guarding all of Jerusalem. So in John's Gospel the whole Roman Army has been turned out to capture this one peaceable man.

I cannot find an image with 800 soldiers, most are a pic-and-mix of the Gospels with soldiers and Temple guards. This has soldiers but in John's account Judas does not kiss Jesus. Actually I must tell you what happens in John's Gospel while this massive army arrests Jesus. Instead of the revealing kiss by Judas, we have Jesus ask:

"Whom do you seek?"
They answered, "Jesus the Nazarene."
He said to them, "I am He."
When He said this they drew back and fell to the ground.
(John 18:4)

I love this, 800 soldiers stagger back and fall to the ground. Would be great in films, but it is never shown.

Remember this contradiction about the Roman soldiers while we move on to the other weird aspect of the arrest. After Jesus is captured he is taken to the High Priest. In Mark's Gospel this High Priest is unnamed.

'They took Jesus to the high priest, and all the chief priests, the elders and the teachers of the law came together.' (14:53)

As Matthew and Luke are just re-writes of Mark, one wonders where they got the name of the High Priest to insert into their versions.

'Those who had seized Jesus led him away to Caiaphas, the High Priest, where the scribes and the elders were gathered together.' (Matthew 26:57)

Okay let us assume they got the name 'Caiaphas' from their research. But we now have a problem; the original Gospel of Mark has no name for the High Priest, Matthew and Luke name Caiaphas, but John's Gospel has a totally different name for the High Priest.

'The Roman cohort and the commander and the officers of the Jews, arrested Jesus and bound him, and led him to Annas first. The High Priest then asked Jesus about his disciples and his doctrine. "Why do you ask me? Ask those who have heard me." And when He had said this, one of the officers struck Jesus with his hand, saying, "Do you answer the High Priest like that?" (John 18:12)

You can look up the High Priests of Israel going right back to the mists of time and there have never been two at the same time, but look how, at the opening of Luke's Gospel, we are introduced to the idea of two High Priests.

'During the High-priesthood of Annas and Caiaphas, the word of God came to John son of Zechariah in the wilderness.'
(Luke 3:2)

Although this quite clearly states there are two High Priests, there is a flakey explanation given by the Church that says there were NOT two High Priests. Annas it declares was the High Priest from AD 6 to 15, which is true, but he was so influential, that he was still called High Priest even after his son-in-law; Caiaphas became High Priest in AD 18. So one is an official High Priest, Caiaphas, and the other Annas, is an old man who was so influential, that he was still called High Priest even after he left office. But I don't buy any of it! Firstly let me repeat Luke's statement:

'In the fifteenth year of the reign of Tiberius Caesar [AD 29] when Pontius Pilate was governor of Judea, Herod tetrarch of Galilee, during the high-priesthood of Annas and Caiaphas, the word of God came to John son of Zechariah.' (Luke 3:1)

This is quite clear; the Bible says there were two High Priests; no ifs or buts; and it places Annas first as if he was the real High Priest! So the modern justification is a total supposition and clearly nonsense. Think about it, Annas had five sons who were High Priests before and after Caiaphas, but low and behold, they are never, ever said to be functioning with Annas as High Priest at the same time, only with this son-in-law, Caiaphas!

And that is not the only odd thing about these High Priests. The name introduced to us by Matthew and Luke, 'Caiaphas' is again total nonsense. There has never ever been a High Priest Caiaphas in the history of Israel. If you look in the encyclopedia at the list of High Priests of Israel, you get this for Annas:

'Annas – the son of Seth, High Priest from AD 6–15.'

Which is true, and for Caiaphas you get this:

 'Caiaphas – properly called Joseph son of Caiaphas was High Priest from AD 18–36, who had married the daughter of Annas.'

Every High Priest is called by his given name, Joshua, Simon, Jonathan, but Caiaphas is not! He is the only High Priest, and I mean the only one in the history of Israel, who is called by his father's name. He should be called High Priest Joseph not Caiaphas; otherwise Jesus would be called Joseph! And John the Baptist would be called Zechariah the Baptist! It is clearly nonsense. Even more significantly, all mention of High Priest Joseph in Josephus' books has been changed to Caiaphas.

'Caiaphas became a high priest during a turbulent period.' (Josephus Antiquities)

Josephus' family were high enough in the establishment to personally know Caiaphas and his son High Priest Joseph so there is no way he would make this mistake and state that this High Priest was called Caiaphas. Somebody must have inserted this into Josephus. What about the church's explanation, that declares that Annas was the High Priest, but he was so influential, that he was still called High Priest even after his son-in-law, Caiaphas became High Priest. The problem is Caiaphas was not the son-in-law of Annas, that was his son Joseph. You see how ridiculous the church's explanation is, almost as ridiculous as Luke claiming there were two High Priests.

In Luke and Matthew, Jesus is taken to High Priest Caiaphas, who was never High Priest and in John's Gospel he is taken to High Priest Annas who also was not High Priest at that time as he relinquished the post in 15 AD.

But just in case you still think this is just confusion by the witnesses and not a clear attempt to conceal something, just follow Peter after the arrest of Jesus.

'Peter had followed him at a distance, right into the courtyard of the high priest, Caiaphas; and he was sitting with the officers and warming himself at the fire.' (Mark 14:53)

As Jesus is questioned by the Sanhedrin, Peter is by the fire in Caiaphas courtyard where he denies Jesus three times:

'Now as Peter was below in the courtyard, one of the servant girls of the high priest came. And when she saw Peter warming himself, she looked at him and said, "You were with that Nazarene Jesus."
But he denied it, saying, "I neither know nor understand what you are saying." And he went out on the porch, and a rooster crowed. And the servant girl saw him again, and began to say to those who stood by, "This is one of them." But he denied it again.' (Mark 14)

The same continues in Matthew and Luke:

'After a little while, those standing there went up to Peter and said, "Surely you are one of them; your accent gives you away."
Then he began to call down curses, and he swore to them, "I don't know the man!"
Immediately a rooster crowed. Then Peter remembered the word Jesus had spoken.'

Pretty straight forward, Peter denies Jesus by a fire in the courtyard of High Priest Caiaphas.

But then comes John's Gospel who has Jesus arrested:

'They bound him and brought him first to Annas'

Peter again follows but to the courtyard of Annas:

'Simon Peter was following Jesus, and so was another disciple. Now that disciple was known to the high priest, and entered with Jesus into the court of the high priest, but Peter was standing at the door outside. So the other disciple, who was known to the high priest, went out and spoke to the doorkeeper, and brought Peter in. Now the slaves and the officers were standing there, having made a charcoal fire.'

So John's Gospel has Peter warming himself by the fire in the courtyard of High Priest Annas, not Caiaphas, where he then denies Jesus.

'Now Simon Peter was standing and warming himself. So they said to him, "You are not also one of his disciples, are you?" He denied it.' (John 18:19)

What is going on? They both cannot be right. So the crucial question is, who was the actual High Priest at the time of Jesus? I do suspect John's version is the truth because of the strange story of the un-named disciple who is, known by the High Priest and is able to wander round his palace and open the door to Peter. There is in fact another mention of Annas being High Priest. Just after the resurrection, Peter and John are brought to trial and in Acts of the Apostles we get this:

'The next day the rulers, the elders and the teachers of the law met in Jerusalem. Annas the High Priest was there, and so were Caiaphas, John, Alexander and others.' (Acts 4:6)

So Annas is clearly stated to be the High Priest at this time, whereas Caiaphas is just present (or inserted later). Surely if Caiaphas was the real High Priest he would be given the title, not Annas who is just supposed to be an influential old man. As I mentioned before, the same is true of Luke's statement: *'Pontius Pilate was governor of Judea, Herod tetrarch of Galilee, during the high-priesthood of Annas and Caiaphas'*. Surely if Caiaphas was the real High Priest his name would come first following the title.

So you will notice in all stories and films, Caiaphas is emphasized as being the High Priest. And as with the other parallel stories I am suggesting the Annas story is the real one and the Caiaphas story is fake. But how can I suggest Annas is the real High Priest who was involved with Jesus when he was High Priest only from 6 to 15 AD when Jesus was a boy? And why are the authorities so determined to suggest Caiaphas is High Priest? Yet I know for certain it was not High Priest Caiaphas, as Caiaphas was never High Priest, nor was he Annas' son in law.

Not only that but I even reject that High Priest Joseph, the son of Caiaphas was the one who dealt with Jesus, even though his tenure was from 18 to 36 AD. I am certain it was High Priest Annas and there is an extraordinary answer to this puzzle, but it requires a full understanding of the history of Israel and Rome at that time.

Chapter Seventeen

THE JEWS IN ROME

Now let us unravel these three contradictions by studying events in Rome at the time. There are several mentions of Jews in Rome by the Jewish historian Josephus who went to Rome before the War of 66 and finally settled in Rome after the war where he wrote his three books. Most of his stories about Jews in Rome are about minor misdemeanors that Jews were involved in and brought discredit on the nation. We will return to these later. Another writer who mentions the Jews in Rome is Suetonius in his book *'The Twelve Caesars'*; his chapter on Claudius has this:

'Since the Jews constantly made disturbances at the instigation of Chrestos, he expelled them from Rome.' (Suetonius)

Here is the actual Latin as this is important:

'Iudaeos impulsore Chresto assidue tumultuantis Roma expulit.'

As this was originally quoted to prove the existence of Jesus we must first consider if this is an original statement or an interpolation by Christians at a later date. Most present day scholars consider this is genuine because, a Christian interpolator would be unlikely to call Jesus 'Chrestos' or a 'troublemaker'. And he could not have influenced Jews in Rome as early as 49 AD. In fact when Paul arrives in Rome thirteen years later, in 62 AD, at his first visit to a synagogue there, the Jews say they have heard of Jesus but have no idea what he was about. Furthermore the expulsion of the Jews is actually mentioned in the Bible but it does not associate the expulsion with Jesus.

'There he (Paul) met a Jew named Aquila, a native of Pontus, who had recently come from Italy with his wife Priscilla, because Claudius had ordered all Jews to leave Rome.' (Acts 18:2)

So there was a Jew, called 'Chrestos', not Christos, who was influential amongst Roman Jews, causing them to make trouble. But Chrestos is not a name, it actually means *'auspicious'*. So this person who is causing the Jews to make trouble is considered by the Jews to be auspicious!

These followers of Chrestos must have been doing something serious to get the whole lot expelled. Perhaps we are talking about someone like Osama bin Laden who influenced Muslims in England and America to cause trouble: enough trouble for President Trump to consider banning the entry of Muslims into the United States.

Whoever this person called Chrestos was, he was obviously very famous to the Jews, someone more famous than Jesus but clearly functioning before Jesus for his fame to reach Rome by 49 AD. So why don't we know who he was? Was his name removed? Or was it never given? And why does Josephus not mention this important event?

Let us now look at another Roman writer, Tacitus, who mentions Christ when writing about the Great Fire of Rome in 64 AD.

'Nero fastened the guilt and inflicted the most exquisite tortures on a class hated for their abominations, called Christians by the populace. Christus, from whom the name

had its origin, suffered the extreme penalty during the reign of Tiberius at the hands of one of our procurators, Pontius Pilatus, and a most mischievous superstition, thus checked for the moment.' ('Annals' Tacitus)

So we have here a clear statement by Tacitus that Pontius Pilate killed Christus and clearly no Christian would describe their religion as a *'most mischievous superstition'*, so we can be reasonably certain that this is a genuine statement by Tacitus. This one statement is why Academics who accept my timeline, push the date of the crucifixion back to 36 AD while Pilate was still in Judea. I have to admit they have every reason not to believe my date of 38 AD and refuse to accept my allegation that Pontius Pilate never crucified Jesus.

But let us be absolutely clear, there definitely was a killing of someone by Pilate, but it does not say this person's name is Jesus or that he was crucified.

'Christus, from whom the name had its origin, suffered the extreme penalty during the reign of Tiberius at the hands of one of our procurators, Pontius Pilatus.'

You see it does not say crucifixion it says extreme penalty. And the official method of Capital punishment was beheading, and for slaves, impaling. It also does not say Jesus either. You may think it is self-evident that it is Jesus, but Christ is just supposed to mean, the anointed one, the Messiah, and there were quite a lot of people claiming to be the Messiah. Look at this from the *Pseudo-clementine Recognitions*:

'Some of the disciples of John (the Baptist), who seemed to be great, have separated themselves from the people, and proclaimed their own master as Christ.' (Recognitions LIV).

So, as John Cleese says in Life of Brian, *"He is the Messiah, and I should know I've followed a few"*. There were plenty of Jews at the time claiming to be King of the Jews, therefore Messiahs or anointed ones.

'Now Judea was full of robbers who lighted on anyone to head them, he was crowned a king immediately in order to do mischief to the public' (Josephus Antiquities)

And there are even more; a Simon, who Josephus says was *'so bold as to put a diadem on his head, and those around declared him to be King.'* Then there was the tall, Athronges, who again wore a diadem and *'this man retained his power a great while.'* Therefore all these can be called Christ, especially if they were anointed, which we know Jesus was not!

Okay, you think I am clutching at straws, and I accept your skepticism, but there is one other aspect of Tacitus statement that may surprise you. Strangely, no Christian quotes Tacitus famous account of Nero's persecution of Christians till the fifteenth century! Why? Surely those early church fathers who quoted many obscure sources, to give evidence to the Jesus story, would have seen Tacitus as manna from heaven.

Perhaps I can tell you one reason it did not surface earlier; it looks like it did not actually say *Christians* at all. Look at what George Andresen noticed in the earliest extent, eleventh century, copy of Tacitus, *Annals*. After the 'i' in Christians there is a strange gap suggesting that the text had been altered, from an 'e'. At first this was ridiculed as nonsense, but then using ultra-violet examination of the manuscript the alteration was conclusively shown.

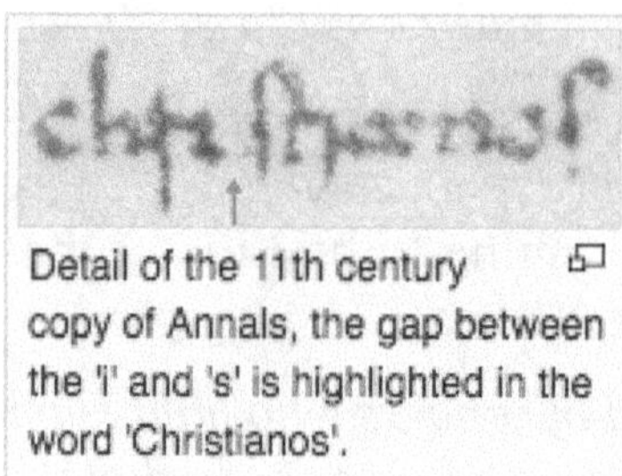

Detail of the 11th century copy of Annals, the gap between the 'i' and 's' is highlighted in the word 'Christianos'.

So it looks like Tacitus used the same term as Suetonius for the person he says suffered 'the extreme penalty' by Pilate. And Nero persecuted this same group of Jewish troublemakers as Claudius, for fanning the flames of the Great Fire of Rome. And now the Tacitus statement makes sense: "*a class hated for their abominations, called Chrestians.*" Why hate peaceful Christian Jesus followers! That makes no sense, but hating vicious Chrestos followers does.

Are we getting close to the persistent, but garbled story of 'a substitute?' Did Pilate not kill Christos the '*anointed*' one, but Chrestos the '*auspicious*' one? And is the impossible date of the crucifixion 32 AD which has been sold to us for centuries, impossible for Jesus but not for Chrestos.

But who was this infamous Jewish troublemaker called Chrestos?

Chapter Eighteen

WHO WAS CHRESTOS?

*'Since the Jews constantly made disturbances at the
instigation of Chrestos, Claudius expelled them from Rome.'*

Let us now explain why the contradictions in the Gospels
relate to the real name of Chrestos.

Contradiction one has Jesus functioning in Galilee and
collecting his disciples by the Sea of Galilee, who leave their
employ on a whim. But this is flatly contradicted in another
Gospel that has Jesus functioning in Judea where he collects
the same disciples who are followers of the Baptist, and
take days to decide to join Jesus.

Contradiction two has the Jews not allowed to stone
people but this is contradicted by several stoning events
before and after this statement.

Contradiction three has Jesus arrested by Jews sent from
the Chief Priests, which is contradicted by an arrested by
the full Roman Jerusalem garrison.

Contradiction four has Jesus accused of blasphemy but
when brought before Pilate he is accused of not paying
taxes and claiming to be king of the Jews, which does not
follow the text of Mark where no such claim is made by him.

And contradiction five has on arrest, Jesus being brought
before High Priest Caiaphas while in another Gospel he is
brought before High Priest Annas.

While these are not the only contradiction that suggest
two separate people being talked about, they are the most
obvious. So if the peace loving Christos is one of these

people, is the militant Chrestos, the auspicious one, the other? Was Jesus the person functioning in Judea while Chrestos was functioning in Galilee? Was the mystic Jesus arrested by Temple guards on a charge of blasphemy, while, the militant Chrestos was arrested by the Cohort of Roman soldiers and taken to Pilate on a charge of refusing to pay taxes and claiming to be king of the Jews?

Surely Chrestos must have been a really famous Jewish militant, somehow associated with Galilee. He must have had a massive following, as his ideas and fame spread all the way to Rome, where his militant followers caused enough trouble in AD 49 for Jews to be banished by Claudius. He also needs to start functioning at least twenty years before Claudius to have time to spread his ideas throughout Israel and then on to the Jews of Rome. And he must have refused to pay Roman tax and claim to be King of the Jews?

Would you believe, there is such a person who fits this profile perfectly! Look at the man Josephus tells us was a claimant to the throne, who started spreading his message thirty years before Claudius in 6 AD. He writes:

'The nation was infected with his doctrine'
'He was a clever Rabbi'
"He stated they were cowards if they would endure to pay a tax to the Romans."
'He was author of the fourth branch of Jewish philosophy.'
'He stirred his followers to rebellion and Josephus claims he was responsible for the war.
'They [his followers] have an inviolable attachment to liberty, and say that God is to be their only Ruler and Lord.'

'They do not value dying any kinds of death, nor indeed do they heed the deaths of their relations and friends, nor can any such fear make them call any man lord.'

A clever rabbi who begins functioning in 6 AD; who was against paying taxes to the Romans, who created a whole new branch of Jewish Philosophy, which spread like wild fire; whose followers believe in an afterlife, which means they face death as martyrs and do not call any ruler Lord. On top of all this our man is often referred to simply as, the Galilean! This has to be Judah the Galilean or often referred to as Judas the Galilean.

With this information you must wonder what the academic world has to say about Judas the Galilean. Here are two extraordinary statements from Encyclopedias about him.

'Judas was a Jewish leader who led an armed resistance to the census imposed for Roman tax purposes by Quirinius in Judaea Province around 6 AD. The revolt was crushed brutally by the Romans. These events are discussed by Josephus in his book 'Jewish Wars.' (Wikipedia)

And this from the Jewish Encyclopedia.

[Judas was] 'leader of a popular revolt against the Romans at the time when the first census was taken in Judea, in which revolt he perished and his followers were dispersed.' (Jewish Encyclopedia)

As you may have noticed I have become very disenchanted with information in encyclopedias during my research on subjects relating to Jesus, but these statements are truly extraordinary! What is so extraordinary? Well there is hardly a word of these supposed expert opinions, that is true, except perhaps:

'These events are discussed by Josephus in his book, 'The Jewish War.'

Yes, they are discussed by Josephus but not in the *'Jewish War'* book, but more so in his book *'Antiquities'* and anyway in no book by Josephus can one find that he:

'led an armed resistance to the census'.

Or

'The revolt was crushed brutally by the Romans.'

Or

'In which revolt he perished and his followers were dispersed.'

Check any encyclopedia and you will get the same fabrications, but the question is why? What is there in the story of Judas the Galilean that is causing this odd state of affairs? Is it just bad and sloppy research? If it is sloppy research it has to be very sloppy because there are only some ten pages in Josephus that mention the Galilean, so if you cannot read ten pages and transcribe them correctly you have to be either pretty dumb, or blind, or very deceitful.

So how did this nonsense end up in the encyclopedias? Let me start by making it clear what the two well-known books by Josephus are all about. Around 72 AD, at the end of the Jewish war, Josephus left Israel and went to live in Rome. He had started as a leader of the Jews and had switched sides to become a favorite of General Vespasian who had captured him. Vespasian left the war to become Emperor while Titus, his son, executed the last two acts of the war, the siege of Jerusalem, which resulted in the destruction of the Temple and then the siege of Masada, which was ended by a mass suicide of the occupants. So one can see why Josephus high tailed it out of Israel to go and live in Rome, in a house supplied by his benefactor, Emperor Vespasian.

In Rome, Josephus wrote up his experiences in the war and included a build up from the time of Pompey's conquest of Jerusalem in 63 BC, which spelled the incorporation of Israel as a client kingdom of the Roman Empire.

In 75 AD Josephus, being annoyed at other writings about the Jewish war, translated his own work into Greek complaining in the Preface:

'While some men who were not concerned in the affairs themselves have gotten together vain and contradictory stories by hearsay; and even those that were present have given false accounts of things, either out of flattery to the Romans, or of hatred towards the Jews. I have myself, for the sake of those that live under the government of the Romans, translated my book into Greek, which I formerly composed in the language of our country. (Josephus Preface)

So this is his first book published in 75 AD in Rome. He had, at this time, no idea of writing another, but twenty years later he did write another, *'The Antiquity of the Jews'*, a general history of the Jewish nation going right back to the story of Adam and Eve and finishing at the War in 66 AD. Now we must be absolutely clear on one thing, the *'War'* book and *'Antiquities'* book both actually contain material from the overlapping dates, 4 BC to 66 AD. Sometimes it appears that he has virtually copied sections from his *'War'* book and placed them in *'Antiquities'*. While the crucial dates of 4 BC to 66 AD are the essence of the *'War'* book they are just passing moments in the *'Antiquities'* book, so one expects that the *'War'* book will cover these dates in far more detail. That said we must firstly take every mention of Judas the Galilean in the 'War' book as stand alone information and consider afterwards what Josephus wrote ten years later in the '*Antiquities*' book.

So here is the first reference to Judas the Galilean in the 'War' book.

And now Archelaus's part of Judea was reduced into a province, and Coponius, one of the equestrian order among the Romans, was sent as a procurator, having the power of death put into his hands by Caesar. It was under his administration that a certain Galilean, whose name was Judas, prevailed with his countrymen to revolt, and said they were cowards if they would endure to pay a tax to the Romans and would after God submit to mortal men as their lords. This man was a teacher of a <u>peculiar sect of his own</u>, and was not at all like the rest of those their leaders.
 For there are three philosophical sects among the Jews. The followers of the first are the Pharisees; the second, the Sadducees; and the third sect are called Essenes. (Bk 2: Ch 8)

So that's it! That is all we have directly about the activities of Judas the Galilean in the '*War*' book. It does not say he led an armed revolt, or that it was put down brutally by the Romans – No it just says that he – '*prevailed with his countrymen to revolt, and said they were cowards if they would endure to pay a tax to the Romans.'*

At this point we have no idea what form this revolt against paying Roman tax took, it may have been *an armed revolt* as the experts writing the encyclopedias state, but that is total speculation. And it does not say *the revolt was put down ruthlessly by the Romans* – again it may have been but this again is pure speculation on the part of the encyclopedia writers. Furthermore Josephus does not write that Judas the Galilean died in that revolt. There is not a single word about him dying here or anywhere in Josephus. For all we know he may have died of old age in bed, because the next reference to him is some sixty years later at the beginning of the war in 66 AD when Josephus writes about Judas' son, Menachem.

"Menachem, son of Judas the Galilean, the very clever rabbi who at the time of Quirinius had reproached the Jews for submitting to the Roman's instead of serving God alone.' (Josephus JW)

So Judas reproached Jews for paying the Roman tax – still no hint of an armed rebellion, but more importantly could this Galilean, be more than 'a *clever rabbi*' as Josephus always refers to him; could he actually be '*auspicious,*' or in Greek, Chrestos? Unfortunately I have never found the name Chrestos linked with the Galilean's name; but then I cannot find *any* Jewish leader linked to the name. Chrestos has to be somebody, as time-wise he just cannot be Jesus, as even Acts of the Apostles does not link the Jews ejected from Rome with Jesus.

'Aquila, a native of Pontus, who had recently come from Italy with his wife Priscilla, because Claudius had ordered all Jews to leave Rome.' (Acts 18:1-2)

So these eighty words are the story of the Galilean in the *'War'* book, clearly that either makes him a very unimportant rebel, or is something missing here? The only difference to other rebels Josephus mentions is that the Galilean had created a new sect, what Josephus calls *'the fourth philosophy of the Jews'* and the original three, he gives as the Pharisees, the Sadducees and the Essenes. Josephus gives us several paragraphs on the beliefs of each of these three sects. But just when you expect to see the fourth philosophy of Judas the Galilean, you get this:

'This is all I wish to say about the philosophic sects.'

Did Josephus really write that? What does it mean? That there is more to tell but he is not going to tell us? Clearly it does not say that is all there is to know about the Jewish sects. Like the lack of any details about the Galilean's life (and death) this abrupt sentence, certainly rings alarm bells that there has been a major cut for some reason.

I should point out here that after this section on the Galilean there is, suspiciously a gap in the *'War'* book of some twenty years before the next event. Did nothing happen of interest between 6 AD and 26 AD? We will investigate these missing years later as they are crucial. Interestingly the event that restarts the narrative in 26 AD is none other than the arrival of Pontius Pilate in Judea.

Luckily towards the end of the *'War'* book, when talking about the siege of Masada, there is another small mention of the Galilean.

*'The fortress of Masada, occupied by the Sicarii under the command of the influential man called Eleazar, a descendent of the Judas who had persuaded many Jews, **as recorded earlier** not to register when Quirinius was sent to Judea to take the census. At that time the Sicarii combined against those prepared to submit to Rome, and in every way treated them as enemies, looting their property, rounding up their cattle, and setting their dwellings on fire: because they declared they were no better than foreigners, throwing away in this cowardly fashion the freedom won by the Jews at such*

cost, and avowedly choosing slavery under the Romans.'
(Josephus bk.7 Ch. 8)

I hope you noticed that Josephus wrote that this was all *recorded earlier* in the book. But you know very well that no such details exist in the book previously. This is all new information about Judas,

*'who had persuaded many Jews, **as recorded earlier** not to register. At that time the Sicarii combined against those prepared to submit to Rome, and in every way treated them as enemies, looting their property, rounding up their cattle, and setting their dwellings on fire.'*

So I think we can safely say that this certainly proves there was a cut in the section on Judas the Galilean and it also confirms that the twenty missing years were not without interest. They were clearly extremely violent and scary, and resulted in the Romans bringing in a different type of Governor to their province of Judea. An inscription found in Caesarea gives Pontius Pilate's title, not as governor but as *Praefectus*, or Prefect, a military term reflecting the fact that the province was turbulent and Pilate's chief task was to bring law and order to the land.

Chapter Nineteen

ANTIQUITIES OF THE JEWS

Perhaps you think Judas' death is not in the 'War' book but in his general book, *'Antiquities of the Jews'* that he wrote fifteen years later. But if it is not in the book about the actual period why would it be in a general book about Jewish history? Surprisingly in *'Antiquities'* there may not be Judas' death but there are interesting details about the twenty missing years, that appear to have been removed from the 'War' book. To make this clear here is my version of the Antiquities book. I tore off the end bit of the book that overlaps the War book so that when I traveled I did not carry the bulk of the book with me, just the period that overlapped to carefully annotate and compare the two.

So you see how few pages there are yet this contains lots more information than the War book about the period 6 AD to 40 AD, and certainly much, much more about Judas the

Galilean and his part in the build up to the war than the 'War' book does. Clearly this is ridiculous!

So first I will reproduce the sections in *'Antiquities'* on the Galilean, which begins with a proper description of who he is, which Josephus probably copied from the 'War' book as he did several other parallel sections, but this is now missing in the War book.

'There was one Judas, a Galilean, of a city whose name was Gamala, who, taking with him Zadok, a Pharisee, became zealous to draw them to a revolt. Both said that this taxation was no better than an introduction to slavery, and exhorted the nation to assert their liberty. They also said that God would not otherwise be assisting to them, than upon their joining with one another in such councils as might be successful, and for their own advantage; and this especially, if they would set about great exploits, and not grow weary in executing the same. So men received what they said with pleasure, and this bold attempt proceeded to a great height.' (Josephus, Antiquities 18.4–6)

A more logical introduction to Judas than what is in the 'War' book. And do you remember this from the War book?

'This is all I wish to say about the philosophic sects.'

Well here Josephus repeats the other three Philosophies and then here is the missing philosophy of Judas the Galilean.

'Judas the Galilean was the author of the fourth branch of Jewish philosophy. These men agree in all other things with the Pharisaic notions (an afterlife); but they have an inviolable attachment to liberty, and say that God is to be their only Ruler and Lord. They also do not value dying any

kinds of death, nor indeed do they heed the deaths of their relations and friends, nor can any such fear make them call any man lord.' (Josephus, Antiquities 18.2–3)

This probably came direct from the War book so why was it cut from there? Later Josephus continues his story as follows:

'All sorts of misfortunes sprang from these men, and the nation was infected with this doctrine to an incredible degree. One violent war came upon us after another, and we lost our friends, which used to alleviate our pains. There were also very great robberies and murder of our principal men. This was done in pretence indeed for the public welfare, but in reality for the hopes of gain to themselves; whence arose seditions, and from them murders of men, which sometimes fell on those of their own people, and sometimes on their enemies. Famine also came upon us, and reduced us to the last degree of despair, as did also the taking and demolishing of cities; nay, the sedition at last increased so high, that the very temple of God was burnt down by their enemies' fire. Such were the consequences of this, that the customs of our fathers were altered, and such a change was made, as added a mighty weight toward bringing all to destruction.' (Josephus, Antiquities 18.7–9)

Again a lot of generalized accusations of murder and mayhem but suspiciously short on detail. However what we can glean is that Judas and his fourth philosophy had a huge following, and he was responsible for; something, that led to mayhem and murder, and which finally brought about the war of 66 AD. So the Galilean was not any old rebel, this is the man who caused the war! The war that Josephus' first book is supposed to be about! So I think we can safely say, that the 'War' book has been butchered to remove the activities of the Galilean and more significantly his death. Why? Josephus always tells us how these people die; he certainly describes the death of two of Judas' sons:

'The sons of Judas of Galilee were now slain: I mean of that Judas who caused the people to revolt, when Quirinius came to take an account of the estates of the Jews, **as we have shown in a foregoing book**.*' (Josephus, Antiqu. 20)*

Surely he hasn't made the same mistake again! Saying it is in the *'War'* book when it is not. Clearly, it was there and it probably explained what these sons did to get themselves killed. But now we have no idea, in fact they are not even mentioned in the *War* book, even though their killing occurred just a dozen years before the war. So we have a clear example of another cut in the War book.

At least we do have mention of these sons dying in 47 AD and we have a description of the death of another son, Menachem, in 66 AD, and we even get a full description of the death of his grandson, Eleazar, in 72 AD. But of the death of Judas the Galilean himself, not a peep.

Remember the 'War' book stood on its own as a description of the build up to the war, the *'Antiquities'* book was not even a twinkle in Josephus' eye. So, the only reason we know something about Judas' philosophy is that the *Antiquities* book covers it, but not the *'War'* book, which basically jumps from the census of 6 AD virtually to the arrival of Pilate, blatantly, skipping some twenty vital years. Vital because Josephus tells us that Joseph ben Caiaphas was made High Priest just before the time of Pilate and adds:

'Caiaphas became a high priest during a turbulent period.'
(Josephus, Antiquities)

What was this *turbulent period* that occurred in those missing years? The book does not say, as opposed to all other turbulent events, Josephus fails to indulge himself in any of the gory details of this event, even though it is the precursors to the very war that his *'War'* book is supposed to be about.

So to recap, we have definite proof that, large chunks about the Galilean were cut from the *War* book. Statements like **'as recorded earlier'** when there is no such thing. Or **'as we have shown in a foregoing book'**, referring to the *War* book, which in fact has far less than the *Antiquities* book about the Galilean.

Given this, I now want to put to you the crucial question. A very simple question that I feel has earth-shattering implications, and I am not exaggerating. The question is - why? Why would anyone tamper with Josephus and edit out information about Judas the Galilean? It is quite obvious why the Baptist would be cut out of the book, and it is equally obvious why James would be cut if Josephus had written things that disagreed with the biblical story. But, why cut out the activities of Judas the Galilean, who superficially has absolutely nothing at all to do with the Jesus story? There can only be one reason and that is, that the Galilean's story *does* contradict some important element of the Gospel story. I challenge anybody to give me any other possible, logical reason why the Judas story has been filleted from the *War* book? There is none, it can only be that Judas the Galilean's story has something that clashes dramatically with the Gospel story! And it is clearly something of very great magnitude.

Chapter Twenty

WHO KILLED THE GALILEAN?

One may wonder why all this has not been spotted by the numerous Academics who study ancient Israel, as it is reasonably self-evident. I can only assume that they look at documents for what is written in them, whereas I have been looking at documents for what is not written in them, what must have been there but is now missing. And it is from this method that I have come to the crucial question: in what important way does the Galilean's story contradict the biblical story of Jesus, when superficially there does not appear to be any link between the two characters? I think you might already be contemplating the answer to that question even if, like me, you still can't quite believe it. I must admit as I was researching, I could hardly believe what was unfolding.

But if I can prove that the Galilean did not die in 6 AD, as reported by every encyclopedia, then my hypothesis would be even more likely.

[Judas was] 'leader of a popular revolt against the Romans at the time when the first census was taken in Judea, in which revolt he perished and his followers were dispersed.'
(Jewish Encyclopedia)

No! You know very well that nowhere is it stated in Josephus that Judas perished in the revolt against the census or that, that revolt was brutally suppressed by the Romans. It is not there. So why then is it constantly repeated? Perhaps they are confusing it with another Judas who led an armed rebellion in Sepphoris, which was crushed brutally by the Romans. But that attack was in 3 BC, nearly ten years before the census, so if they killed Judas then, how could he lead the revolt against the census in 6 AD? Furthermore it is not even agreed by all that the Judas who led the Sepphoris attack was in fact our man. (Although I believe it is possible.)

Having read all the versions of Josephus in all the different languages, Academic Robert Eisler concludes:

'The date when Judas (the Galilean) fell and his followers dispersed cannot be precisely fixed, but his work was carried on by his sons.' (Dr. Robert Eisler)

So, why has this story about Judas death in 6 AD been spread, and more importantly, who cares enough about when or how Judas the Galilean died, to spread the fake story of his death in 6 AD? And cared enough to remove his death from Josephus, because it is unthinkable to believe Josephus did not write the death of the man who caused the war in his 'War' book? Perhaps the answer is here:

*'Some time ago Theudas appeared, claiming to be somebody, and about four hundred men rallied to him. He was killed and all his followers were dispersed, and it all came to nothing. **After him**, Judas the Galilean appeared in the days of the census and led a band of people in revolt. He too was killed, and all his followers were scattered.' (Acts 5:36)*

This is the only reference to Judas death at the time of the census but it is also one of the strangest verses in the Holy Bible because whereas there are contradictions between one Gospel and another, this is a total mess within itself. It is supposed to be an account of a speech made by a Pharisee named Gamaliel, when Peter was arrested.

Extraordinarily, he refers to the revolt by Theudas and, after him; another led by our Judas the Galilean. Trouble is, this speech by Gamaliel is happening around 35 AD, but Josephus places Theudas' revolt under Fadus, who became Governor in 44 AD, which is nearly ten years later. So the Theudas's revolt had not yet happened when Gamaliel is supposed to be speaking. Also the revolts of Judas and Theudas are mistakenly reversed Judas should come first and then Theudas. Yet it says *'after him'* came Judas the Galilean. This weird, anachronistic verse from the Bible is supposed to be proof that Judas died at the time of the census. But all that it can possibly prove is that either the person writing this has messed up, big time, or perhaps he is right; Judas arose at the time of the census and his movement was still functioning after the revolt by Theudas in AD 44, which we know it was. It clearly does not actually say that Judas died at the time of the census.

Judas the Galilean appeared in the days of the census and led a band of people in revolt. (Full stop, which could mean any amount of time before) - *He too was killed, and all his followers were scattered* – (perhaps at the time of Pilate!) So even this verse does not tell us when Judas died, yet it is often quoted as saying just that. Here is an example:

*'JUDAS OF GALILEE Mentioned in Acts 5:37 as the leader of an insurrection occasioned by the census of Quirinius in 7 A.D. He, and those who obeyed him, **it is said**, perished in that revolt. (International Standard Bible Encyclopedia)*

'It is said?' By whom? And *perished in that revolt* is a total and utter invention, as it is neither in Josephus, nor even in the Bible, which just says he appeared in 6 AD, full stop, and died sometime. Or of course the other interpretation of this

statement is that the revolt, we know, lasted sixty years from 6 to 66 AD. So the Galilean could have died *'in that revolt'* but it could have been any time in the sixty years.

Unfortunately, around these dates, the very years that Judas and Jesus would be functioning, there is very little in Josephus till this little section, which is not in the *War* book but only in *Antiquities*.

'About this time there lived Jesus, a wise man, if indeed one ought to call him a man. For he was one who performed surprising deeds and was a teacher of such people as accept the truth gladly. He won over many Jews and many of the Greeks. He was the Messiah. And when, upon the accusation of the principal men among us, Pilate had condemned him to a cross, those who had come to love him did not cease. He appeared to them spending a third day restored to life, for the prophets of God had foretold these things and a thousand other marvels about him. And the tribe of the Christians, so called after him, has still to this day not disappeared.' (Josephus, Antiquities)

Okay, this is accepted by all to be a forgery; with *'He was the Messiah'* a very unlikely statement from a Jew, and anyway Josephus claimed his captor and benefactor, the Emperor Vespasian, was the Messiah. He also mentions Christians who are unlikely to exist at such an early date. But actually I believe some of it could be original and Jesus was mentioned. But this is the *'Antiquities'* book, if Jesus was mentioned it would have been in the *'War'* book, which is specifically about the period Jesus was supposed to have functioned.

But this position of Jesus in Josephus just happens to be exactly where I would expect to find the death of Judas the

Galilean. Why? Because there is actually a way of revealing the timing of the Galilean's death, even if we can't exactly say how it happened? Look at this event at the start of the war in 66.

'In the meantime, one Menachem, the son of that Judas, who was called the Galilean, took some of the men of note with him, and retired to Masada, where he broke open King Herod's armory, and gave arms not only to his own people, but to other robbers also.' (Josephus War)

Just work this out: if Judas had this last son, Menachem, say, around AD 30, that would make Menachem around thirty-six when he led this attack on Masada in 66 AD. If that is a likely age for an active rebel leader, then Judas impregnated his wife, not much earlier than AD 28 and not much later than AD 34. Since Pilate was Prefect from AD 26 to 36, the birth of Menachem must have been right in the middle of Pilate's reign. So logically Judas was alive when Pilate arrived but there is no evidence that he was still alive when Pilate left Israel, as it is his sons who are leading the revolt after that date.

Others have spotted this about Menachem and have decided that Josephus did not actually mean *son* so decide to call Menachem a relative of Judas. How desperate is this? Anywhere else, if Josephus says son it is accepted he means son; if he says wife, he means wife; if he says daughter, he means daughter; but in this one place, when he says son, he means relative! But this attempt to confuse still does not matter because two older sons, Simon and Jacob are killed in 48 AD, as reported in *'Antiquities'*. So if they were around 28 years old that still makes them born in 20 AD fourteen years after the supposed death of their father, and nowhere do they deny these two are the Galileans sons. Calling Menachem, Judas' relative instead of son, gives us clear evidence that early Christian forgers noticed this anomaly of the age of Menachem.

Now look at the quote about the leader of the famous siege of Masada.

'Eleazar, a descendent of the Judas, who had persuaded many Jews not to register with the census of Quirinius.'
(Josephus, War)

Actually this is not how the original text went. In the Slavonic version of the *War* book instead of *a descendent* it actually has, *'the grandson'*. I ask you to consider why anyone would be so worried by the term *grandson* that they felt the need to change it to *descendent*?

So between Menachem and Eleazar we have clear evidence that, if Judas had impregnated his wife and then died in 6 AD, that would make Menachem a bit too old to be clambering up to the mountaintop fortress of Masada and whacking the Romans in 68 AD. This attack by Menachem makes the date of his birth somewhere around AD 30, and that would establish somewhere around 32 AD as the most likely date for Judas to have died. And of course this is exactly the date that Jesus is claimed to have been crucified by Pontius Pilate, even though that date looks impossible for Jesus, as John the Baptist was still alive.

Is that still a bit too big a jump of logic for you? Well just remember, when Josephus mentioned the appointment of Caiaphas as High Priest, just before the time of Pilate, he added:

'Caiaphas became a high priest during a turbulent period.'
(Josephus Antiquities)

So the 'turbulent period', seems to have been brought to an end after Caiaphas became High Priest. How? By the appointment of a military Prefect, Pontius Pilate who did something to bring it to an end. And how did Pilate bring this turbulent period to an end? By crucifying the peaceful Jesus? Obviously not! It had to be the destruction of the rebel army and the capture and killing of their leader, Judas the Galilean. And how did Pilate capture Judas? Look at this statement in the Bible:

'It was Caiaphas who had advised the Jewish leaders that it was expedient for one man to die for the people.' (John 18:14)

This is interpreted as Caiaphas recognizing that Jesus was going to die to save our souls; but that is a most unlikely explanation as it makes Caiaphas recognize Jesus as some sort of God-like figure. A much more likely interpretation is the sort of dilemma that faced village leaders in occupied France during the Second World War: either to sacrifice one resistance fighter or have twenty villagers shot. So it looks like Caiaphas is going to betray Judas to the Romans, which would result in the peace that the Jewish authorities required and the peace that Jesus the prophet seemed to be functioning in.

Josephus must have described the betrayal by the High Priest that resulted in the defeat of the rebels and the capture of their leader, but it was cut. Perhaps you think I do not have enough evidence to make such a bold and definitive statement and I accept your skepticism as justified. But let me introduce you to a section of Slavonic Josephus, which looks exactly like my suggestion. Slavonic Josephus is not an uncut version of Josephus, but it still has a few original sections and others that have been so crudely edited that they were later thrown out. Here is one such crudely edited section that was later thrown out. I will <u>underline</u> the Christian interpolations, which you will see are the silly bits.

'They bade him enter the city, kill the Roman troops and Pilate and reign over us. <u>But he did not care to do so</u>. When knowledge of it came to the Jewish leaders, they gathered together with the High priest and spake: "We are powerless and weak to withstand the Romans. But as withal the bow is bent, we will go and tell Pilate what we have heard, and we will be without distress, lest if he hear it from others, we be robbed of our substance and ourselves be put to the sword and our children ruined." And they went and told it to Pilate. And he sent and had many of the people cut down. And brought in <u>the wonder-doer</u>. And when he had instituted a trial concerning him, <u>he perceived that he is a doer of good, but not an evildoer, nor a revolutionary, nor one desirous of kingship, and set him free. He had, you should know, healed his dying wife. And they gave 30 talents to Pilate that they should kill him. And he took it and gave them liberty to carry out their wishes themselves. And they sought out a suitable time to kill him. For they had given Pilate 30 talents earlier, that he should give Jesus up to them. And they crucified him against the ancestral law; and they greatly reviled him.</u> (Slavonic Josephus)

This is what is written in Slavonic Josephus' version of the 'War' book – (and of course our War book has no mention of Jesus) and obviously the whole piece could not be a Christian interpolation because it makes no sense and in fact contradicts the Gospel story. It has to be about an armed leader of a rebellion and the Jesus inserts have been slipped in by a complete idiot. For instance they inform Pilate about *this bad person* to save further bloodshed. Pilate's cohort of soldiers then cut down many of *this person's* followers. But when *this person* is brought to trial, Pilate finds him innocent! This makes the whole event crazy because handing him over, by the Jewish authorities, to save further bloodshed, was a complete waste of time as Pilate has no interest in him because he had done nothing wrong. And even more ridiculous is the bribing of Pilate so that the Jews can crucify Jesus themselves *'against ancestral law'*. This was so silly that it was discarded in the final orthodox version of Josephus *'War'* book and I am not surprised. I must say I particularly like the little bit about Jesus having popped in to cure Pilates' wife. Sadly, in the Bible she just has a boring dream.

The section has got to be about Judas, not Jesus because: *'they bade him* (Jesus? or Judas?) *to enter the city, kill the Roman troops and Pilate and rule over us.'* Surely this could not be about Jesus and there is no event in the Jesus story that has *'And Pilate sent and had many of the people cut down.'* But it does fit perfectly into the Judas story as I am presenting it. The encouragement by the Jews to kill Pilate makes total sense since he had outraged the Jerusalem population by bringing in Roman Standards with craven images, which is reported by Josephus as causing massive commotion, as craven images are absolutely forbidden by Jewish law.

Here is the section as it probably appeared without the silly bits.

'They bade Judas the Galilean to enter the city, kill the Roman troops and Pilate and reign over us. When knowledge of it came to the Jewish leaders, they gathered together with the

High priest and spake: "We are powerless and weak to withstand the Romans. But as withal the bow is bent, we will go and tell Pilate what we have heard, and we will be without distress, lest if he hear it from others, we be robbed of our substance and ourselves be put to the sword and our children ruined." And they went and told it to Pilate. And he sent and had many of the people cut down. And brought in the Galilean. And when he had instituted a trial concerning him, he found him guilty of rebellion and sent him to crucifixion.

Interestingly this ties in perfectly with the quote from the Bible where Caiaphas suggests getting rid of one to save the many and reads exactly how I paralleled it with the French resistance. This surely has to be where Josephus described the capture and death of Judas the Galilean.

I mentioned that this *'bribing of Pilate so that they can crucify Jesus'* was the first crude attempt, to blame the crucifixion of Jesus on to the Jews. How does the Bible finally achieve this?

"Of all the discrepancies, inconsistencies and improbabilities in the Gospels, the choice of Barabbas is among the most striking and most inexplicable. Something would clearly seem to lie behind so clumsy and confusing a fabrication."
(Lincoln, Leigh, Baigent: Holy Blood, Holy Grail)

The Barabbas story is *'inexplicable'* if one does not understand why it was invented, which was to blame the Jews for Jesus' death, and to confuse Jesus and Judas. This is the normal translation of Matthew 27:15.

'Now at the feast the governor was accustomed to release for the people any one prisoner whom they wanted. At that time, they were holding a notorious prisoner, called Barabbas. So when the people gathered together, Pilate said, "Whom do

you want me to release? Barabbas, or Jesus who is called Christ?" (Matthew 27:15)

We cannot actually find any evidence that Roman Governors offered the populace a chance to release one of their convicted criminals. Especially, to make a choice between a blasphemer and a murdering rebel, the exact types, who were crucified by the Romans. So not only is it unlikely but look at the uncut, full translation of Matthew 27:15.

'Pilate said to them, "Whom do you want me to release for you, Jesus Barabbas or Jesus who is called the Messiah?" (Matthew 27:15)

Usually Barabbas' first name is cut out of translations because it looked so strange that his name is Jesus Barabbas! And they saw it as confusing, not realizing that that is exactly why it is there. But even more confusing is that Barabbas actually means *'son of the father'*, so we have a choice to crucify Jesus the Messiah or Jesus son of the father, which clearly could be Jesus himself. Weird or what? If the switch of Judas and Jesus was flagged by those in the know, any questions could be answered with, "Yes you are right; a revolutionary was caught by Pilate, a guy called Jesus Barabbas, but hey, it was at the same time as Jesus the Messiah" and they released Jesus and crucified Jesus. Confusing? Yes and that is the purpose of the Barabbas story that seemed so weird to the writers of 'Holy Blood', which made them wonder if Barabbas, *'son of the rabbi'* could be Jesus' son!

I should add that John 18:40 says Barabbas was a 'robber' but in fact the word used in Greek is *'lestai'*, which is a word used to describe Judas the Galileans zealots.

I would also remind you that in this insertion, the crowd are given a choice between Jesus or Barabbas, but in reality the choice should have been between four criminals, Jesus and Barabbas and the two robbers crucified either side of Jesus, but in their carelessness the forgers forgot all about our two supporting players.

But the worse aspect of this Barabbas event in the Bible is that the crowd are, tragically made to say:

"His blood shall be on us and on our children!" (Mat. 27:23)

We had a crowd speak in unison in 'Life of Brian' and it was funny and very silly causing the audience to laugh in hysterics. But this bit of 'crowd speaking in unison' silliness is the most disastrous sentence in the whole Bible. Can you imagine how self-satisfied those who wrote the Barabbas story were when they repaired, so successfully, the first silly attempt to conceal the switch and blame the Jews. And I have to admit the deception worked brilliantly. It turns my stomach thinking of those smug forgers who are responsible for the murder of millions of Jews.

So I am suggesting Judas was about to launch a raid on Jerusalem and was gathering followers on the Mount of Olives probably responding to a prophesy in Zechariah:

'And his feet shall stand in that day upon the Mount of Olives, which is before Jerusalem on the east.' (Zechariah 14:4)

With the help of God they are getting ready to attack Jerusalem and kill Pilate, but before they can move, Joseph ben Caiaphas the High Priest betrays them to Pilate who turns out the Jerusalem barracks. And it is this cohort of 800 soldiers who attack the rebels, killing many. Judas himself is captured, and taken to jail. The Galilean stands trial before Pilate and is sentenced to death as a rebel who refused to pay Roman tax and claimed to be a king. A sign is pinned saying, 'King of the Jews', which the Chief Priests objected to, exactly as it says in the Bible. His body rots on the stake. After a period of peace, (which is clearly the time Jesus is functioning) when Judas' sons came of age they follow in their father's footsteps and re-ignited the revolt against the Romans. Two of the sons were killed, in 46 AD, but that was edited out of the War book and we only know about them because they appear briefly in the Antiquities book but followed by, *'as we have shown in a foregoing book.'* I state that they re-ignited the rebellion because three years later Claudius expelled the Jews from Rome because of Chrestos. A younger son, Menachem, is involved in the first actions of the war and like Judas the Galilean, acts as a king:

With these as bodyguard he returned to Jerusalem like a King, put himself in charge of the insurgents and took charge of the siege.

Clearly Menachem, like his father, seems to have royal aspirations because Josephus continues with Menachem entering the Temple:

'... in pomp to worship, decked with kingly robes and followed by a train of armed zealots.' (Josephus, War)

After the destruction of Jerusalem and the Temple the final act of the war was led by Judas' grandson Eleazar, who held out on the mountain fortress of Masada till 73 AD.

So Judas the Galilean and his family were absolutely instrumental to the actions that led to the war and there is a very simple reason why so many Jews supported the Galilean, and it relates to the festival of Hanukkah. This Jewish festival celebrates events a hundred years before the

Galilean when his namesake, Judas Maccabeus and his sons succeeded in winning the war of independence over the Greeks, using exactly the same tactics as the Galilean. Judas Maccabeus, beat the Greeks surely Judas the Galilean will beat the Romans too? One can guess the speeches by the militants, "We will win however long it takes and whatever the cost because like Judas Maccabeus, God is with us, his chosen people. We will again free Israel from the oppressors and then we will cleanse the Temple." Just imagine how that would go down during the festival of Hanukkah.

Chapter Twenty-one

HOW DID JESUS DIE?

'Pilate said, "Take him and judge him by your own law."

My timeline claims that when the Baptist was beheaded around 36 AD, Jesus functioned for two years in the relatively peaceable time created by Vitellius. This makes the correct date for Jesus death around 38 AD. So the next question is how did Jesus die? Was he crucified by the Romans? From the evidence it is almost impossible to believe the statement only in John's Gospel:

'Pilate said, "Take him and judge him by your own law."
"But we have no right to execute anyone," they objected.
(John 18:31)

So the Sanhedrin were not allowed to stone blasphemers, but as mentioned, almost immediately after the death of Jesus, Stephen is stoned to death. And don't forget the well-known story where Jesus protects a prostitute with, "Let him who has not sinned throw the first stone." But we are supposed to believe nobody is allowed to stone anyone – "Even if they do say, Jehovah" - as was portrayed in the stoning scene in 'Monty Python's Life of Brian'.

Clearly the Sanhedrin had no need to take Jesus to the Roman Governor, for him to carry out the sentence, especially as blasphemy has nothing at all to do with the Romans and even in the story, Pilate seems to be reluctant to carry out the sentence. Clearly both Stephen and Peter in Acts, accuse the Sanhedrin of being the killers.

'The God of our ancestors raised Jesus from the dead – whom you killed by hanging him on a tree.'

And we know hanging on a tree is part of the stoning ritual.

'If a man guilty of a capital offense is put to death and his body hung on a tree, you must not leave his body on the tree overnight. Be sure to bury him that same day, because anyone who is hung on a tree is under God's curse.' (Deuteronomy 21:22)

Obviously it is hard to believe that Jesus was stoned by the Jews and not crucified by the Romans but could the stoning of Jesus actually still be in the Bible. Look at Acts 10:39 which is translated sometimes as:

"We are witnesses of all the things He did both in the land of the Jews and in Jerusalem. They also put Him to death by hanging Him on a cross.' (Acts 10:39)

The correct translation does not say 'cross'. Look how the correct translation reads:

'Whom they slew and hung on a tree.' (King James translation)

So in this correct translation he is slain before he is hung on a tree as with stoning. Not killed by hanging on a tree or a cross. Has this slipped through the editing process to reveal a truth? And Peter actually accuses the Sanhedrin of Jesus death.

'The God of our ancestors raised Jesus from the dead – whom you killed by hanging him on a tree." (Acts 5:30)

Peter is definitely suggesting the Sanhedrin are, not just accomplices, but the actual perpetrators. That begins to raise the question as to why the Sanhedrin would take Jesus to Pilate and accuse him, of claiming to be King of the Jews, which is not a claim Jesus makes in any of the two original Gospels, Mark and John. Or more to the point why not take him to the actual King, Herod who will soon chop his head off, as he did John the Baptist, for questioning his legitimacy and claiming to be the rightful king.

Furthermore why does the Jewish Talmud state that Jeschu was stoned to death?

'The Sages of the Synagogue, succeeding in capturing Jeschu, who was then led before the Great and Little Sanhedrin, by whom he was condemned to be stoned to death and his dead body was hung on a tree.' (Talmud)

What possible reason could they have for making this monumental mistake, which would only discredit the early part of the document? And why would Jews put the blame for Jesus death, fairly and squarely on their own shoulders? But this is not just a one off document, another reads:

'On the eve of Passover Jesus, the Nazarene was hanged and a herald went forth before him forty days heralding, 'Jesus the Nazarene is going forth to be stoned because he practiced sorcery and instigated and seduced Israel to idolatry.
(Babylonian Sanhedrin 43a–b)

Besides agreeing on his death, both documents clearly accept that the Sanhedrin can stone people, adding to all the other evidence that contradicts the one solitary statement in John's Gospel, that the Sanhedrin can't stone people.

We even have the early Jewish critic of Christianity, Celsus who is mentioned by Origen as repeating:

*'Although Celsus becomes tautological in his statements about Jesus, repeating for a second time that, "**he was punished by the Jews for his crimes,**" we shall not again take up the defense.' (Origen 'Contra Celsus Bk2 Ch5')*

So it appears Celsus keeps repeating to the Christians that it was the Jews who killed Jesus not the Romans. It is a pity we have not got his original statement because it probably said he was stoned by the Jews not crucified by the Romans.

This deception seems to be the origin of the Dark Ages. When the Christian religion was adopted by the Roman Empire around 330 AD it resulted in the mass murder of the original Christians the torture of others, the destruction of books and the re-writing of others, all to sell Paul and Luke's version of the truth. We know for certain what sections were inserted into key books like Josephus. These are even admitted by Christian scholars. We know that it must have been them who changed Chrestos to Christos in Tacitus statement because it was never quoted as a proof of Jesus before the Middle Ages. And don't forget how early Christians even tampered with Suetonius to forge the name Chrestos into Christos as well. Luckily there were surviving copies that had not been tampered with.

But the real question is not what they added but what did they cut out? And most importantly what did they cut out of the books of Josephus?

It is almost certain that they cut the death of, the most famous Jew repeatedly mentioned by Josephus, Judas the Galilean. It is almost impossible to believe the Galileans death was not there especially as Josephus writes, Judas is responsible for the whole war his book is about, but then forgets to tell us how and when Judas died but does remember to tell us how his sons died and even his grandson.

Another major event involving the Jews is mentioned in both Suetonius and the Bible, the expulsion of the Jews from Rome ten years before the war.

'After this Paul left Athens and went to Corinth. There he fund a Jew named Aquila, a native of Pontus, who had recently come from Italy with his wife Priscilla, because Claudius had ordered all Jews to leave Rome.' (Acts 18:1-2)

And from Suetonius.

'Since the Jews constantly made disturbances at the instigation of Chrestus, he [the Emperor Claudius] expelled them from Rome.'

So why is this major Jewish event just before the war, not in the books of Josephus? Obviously because it told us the name of this important Jew, Chrestus who was responsible for the expulsion of the Jews from Rome.

While Europe was burning books and re-writing others, in the Islamic world books were being collected and translated. There was the famous 'House of Wisdom' established by the Caliph of Bagdad and of course the library of Alexandria, which was finally burnt down by Christians.

We have now explained two of the contradictions in the Bible. The first, why there was an attempt to place Jesus in Galilee when it is clear he functioned in Judea and Jerusalem.

"We are witnesses of all the things He did both in the land of the Jews and in Jerusalem.' (Acts 10:39)

We have also suggested that the statement in John, that the Sanhedrin were not allowed to stone blasphemers is at least questionable. We have yet to explain why John says the High Priest who dealt with Jesus was Annas, while the Synoptic Gospels state the High Priest was Caiaphas, when Caiaphas was never High Priest. I have made the case for Annas being the High Priest even though he relinquished the post in 16 AD when Jesus was a child. There is a fascinating answer to this puzzle that we will unfold once you have a little more information.

Chapter Twenty-two

THE CRUCIFIXION OF JESUS!

'Now in the place where He was crucified there was a garden, and in the garden a new tomb in which no one had yet been laid.' (John 19:41)

I feel I have to return to the crucifixion, as even though I have suggested Jesus was stoned to death, I still believe in the crucifixion. The nature of the crucifixion of Jesus is probably revealed in Clement's letter. Have another look:

'He [Mark] brought in certain sayings of which he knew the interpretation would, as a mystagogue, lead the hearers into the innermost sanctuary of truth hidden by seven veils... being read only by those who are being initiated into the great mysteries. Mark composed a more spiritual Gospel for the use of those being perfected. Nevertheless, he yet did not divulge the things not to be uttered, nor did he write down the Hierophantic teaching of the Lord.'

The letter clearly states that Jesus is a *'hierophant'*, which is an interpreter of sacred mysteries or esoteric principles. And a mystagogue is someone who instructs others before initiation into religious mysteries. Lazarus resurrection is into a higher degree as described in Secret Mark.

'After six days Jesus told him what to do and in the evening the youth comes to him, wearing a linen cloth over his naked body. And he remained with him that night, for Jesus taught him the mystery of the kingdom of God.' (Secret Mark)

John's Gospel tells us that this event is happening in Bethany, so the tomb is in the garden of the home of Mary, Martha and Lazarus. Now just consider the version of the Crucifixion of Jesus in John's Gospel with a few little gems of information that have slipped through the censors.

'Now in the place where He was crucified there was a garden, and in the garden a new tomb in which no one had yet been laid.' (John 19:41)

A garden? How many houses in Jerusalem have gardens? And how many of these have tombs in them, with rolling stone doors? I do know of one exactly like this one, and here it is:

'Jesus went off with her into the garden where the tomb was... And going near Jesus rolled away the stone from the door of the tomb.' (Mark)

And after the Crucifixion, Mark writes:

'They asked each other, 'Who will roll the stone away from the tomb?" But when they looked up, they saw that the stone, which was very large, had been rolled away.' (Mark 16:3)

A garden in Jerusalem is not at all common but one with a rolling stone tomb must be a one off. Surely the Crucifixion of Jesus was not a capital punishment at all, but an initiation ritual taking place in the same garden with the same tomb that was involved in Lazarus' initiation? This place must be close enough to the residence of Mary so that she can run with the news.

Mary Magdalene went to the tomb and saw the stone had been removed from the entrance. So she ran to Simon Peter and the other disciple, the one Jesus loved, and said, "They have taken the Lord out of the tomb, and we don't know where they have put him!" So Peter and the other disciple started for the tomb. Both were running, but the other disciple outran Peter and reached the tomb first. (John 20:1)

Given the distance to where the tombs are in Jerusalem, it is just not feasible for anybody but an Olympic athlete to race the two miles from Bethany, and back? All this suggests this is the same garden and the same tomb in Bethany that was used for the raising of Lazarus. So we must add yet another incident to our list of events occurring in Bethany. We have the anointing, the raising of Lazarus and I suggested that the Last Supper took place in Bethany. And now we have to add the ritual of crucifixion!

Okay, you cannot believe that anyone would actually crucify themselves as part of an initiation into a higher state. No? Well look at the following image; in fact, one of the earliest images of a Crucifixion in the cross shape we recognize.

One would imagine that this is the Crucifixion of Jesus. But the inscription on this plaster cast, of this third century amulet, reads *'Orpheus becomes a Bacchoi'*. To become a Bacchoi, is to become an enlightened disciple. So this event is an initiation. Is this what the Gnostics understood to be the crucifixion, not capital punishment at all but a ritual of death and resurrection?

An initiate into Orphic mysteries is promised advantages in the afterlife. There are many dying and resurrecting Gods. The most illustrious is Dionysus. His name means, the Son of God! Dionysus was torn to pieces by the Titans, but after his death he was resurrected with the help of Goddess Athena. The first forms of theatre were called 'Dithyrambos' and they represented the passion and the resurrection of Dionysus.

All these mysteries telling a story of death and resurrection originate in Egypt and the story of Osiris. So you see there is nothing new in the death and resurrection idea but the mysteries usually have the resurrection after three days in Hades, and in fact Matthew and Luke similarly announces that Jesus will resurrect in three days.

'Thus it stands written that the Christ would suffer and would rise from the dead on the third day. (Luke 24:46)

No, this is not written! Not in the Bible anyway. It appears in the Mystery religions and it looks like Jesus is going to match the Mysteries and stay in the tomb for three days, but does not quite manage it, unless you count Friday evening to Sunday morning three days.

Perhaps you are still not convinced that what happened in the garden was a ritual as opposed to what is supposed to have happened at Golgotha? So read this:

'I know that I hung from that wind swept tree, nine long nights, wounded with a spear, dedicated to [O], myself to myself, of that tree of which no man knows, from where its roots run. No bread did they give me, nor drink from a horn,

downwards I peered, I took up the runes, screaming I took them, then I fell back from there."

The name [O] I removed is in fact Odin! This is a Norse legend from the Havamal, which tells how Odin sacrificed himself on the world tree to challenge death. It ends with:

'These are the words of Odin before there were men. These were his words after his death, when he rose again.'

Odin made his spiritual journey to other dimensions of reality in his search for wisdom. He dies so as to win the occult wisdom possessed only by the dead, and rises again to use that wisdom in the world of the living. I am not asking you to believe this concept; I am just trying to show you the type of thinking behind the ritual. You can find a similar view of initiation in Masonic text.

'He only is worthy of initiation in the profounder mysteries who has overcome the fear of death.' (The Masonic Testament)

Perhaps this very early image of a cross-formed Crucifixion can help. It is the Alexamenos graffiti, a carving on a pillar in Rome, which shows a donkey headed man, crucified.

What could it mean? Obviously some wit could be ridiculing the Christians for worshipping the instrument of his death. But why the donkey head?

There is a dualist belief from the mystery religions that the Gnostics took up. The idea is that within yourself you have opposites, a lower and higher self, the Eidolon and the Daemon. Initiation leads to the overcoming of your lower self. The ass was a symbolic representation of your lower eidolon, and in the mystery religion the Godhead rides on a donkey while the crowd wave palm leaves, signifying his dominance over, his lower self, represented by the donkey. So perhaps nailing your carnal body to the four arms of a cross, symbolically releases your Daemon leaving your lower self, (the donkey) attached.

Initiates would understand the cross as an instrument to pin your lower self to. Could that explain why the Knights Templars spat on the cross, as it contained your lower eidolon? Without initiation into these ideas one can easily see how it can all get very confusing. The original Christians were often accused of cannibalism for eating the body of Jesus and drinking his blood, because critics took the Eucharist literally.

So, Jesus' Crucifixion could also be a misinterpretation of an occult ceremony and like the Orpheus cross the form was nothing to do with Roman punishment. Certainly the Gnostic Christians believed it to be with their statement:

'Christ Crucified is teaching for babes.'

Or should we say:

'Christ crucified is teaching for the uninitiated.'

And remember, the Gnostic Christians were very early Christians, much earlier and probably more in tune with the ideas of Jesus than the Roman Orthodox Church whose authority over the Jerusalem Church comes from the power of the Roman army, not from any reasoned argument.

But why were the initiates of Orpheus using what appears to be the same instrument for their rituals as used for capital punishment by the Romans, an elaborately constructed four arm cross? The answer is that the Romans never used crucifixion as a method of Capital punishment. This is probably one of the most controversial statements I have made in this book. Remember the Tacitus statement that was supposed to confirm that 'Jesus was crucified by Pilate'.

'Nero fastened the guilt and inflicted the most exquisite tortures on a class hated for their abominations, called Christians by the populace. Christus, from whom the name had its origin, suffered the extreme penalty during the reign of Tiberius at the hands of one of our procurators, Pontius Pilatus, and a most mischievous superstition, thus checked for the moment.' ('Annals' Tacitus)

If you remember at the time I pointed out that it never said *'Jesus'* and it never mentioned *'crucifixion'*. It just said *'Christus'* and *'the extreme penalty. '* And I said I would later show that the *extreme penalty* was not crucifixion. As it is going to take many, many pages of proof to convince you I am not bonkers, for now let me suggest one possible reason the ritual used crucifixion and I will deal with the Romans and the *'extreme penalty'* in a later chapter.

Could the four arms of the cross relate to the four elements, earth, air, fire and water. This may sound a little insignificant now but the concept held much weight in ancient times. This I found in one book.

'This connection exists between the cross and Alchemy. In common Chemistry, says Pernetz, crosses form characters, which indicate the crucible, vinegar and distilled vinegar. But as regards hermetic science.... the cross is the symbol of the four elements.'

You can find the four elements symbolized throughout history, for instance even in this late painting of 'Christ Crowned with Thorns' by Hieronymus Bosch.

These four human types, surrounding Jesus, represent the four elements, air, earth, fire and water, each associated with the relevant astrological part of the body. Air, top right, with a stave to thrust Jesus up into the air and touching the shoulder, the very part of the body associated with the air sign Gemini. Fire, the choleric, with iron fist, the metal of Mars that rules over Aries, associated with the head, on which he thrusts the crown. Water, the phlegmatic type with lewd gesture towards Jesus, linked to the Zodiacal Scorpio, the water sign that rules over the sexual organs. Then the Earth type, the melancholic, who pulls

Jesus down into the dark earth of the grave. The concept of earth, air, fire and water has been all-pervasive since Plato coined the phrase 'the four elements'. In the Mystery religions people were baptized in the elements. A winnowing fan is used for air and, lo and behold, it appears in the Bible, where John the Baptist says:

'I indeed baptize you with water unto repentance, but He who is coming after me is mightier than I. He will baptize you with the Holy Breath and fire. His winnowing fan is in his hand.' (Matthew 3:11)

So the even-armed cross could well have arisen as a symbol of the four elements.

I offer that as one possible theory, but it is not the one I favor. There was one heretical group that we have no evidence of other than from the attacks by Church Fathers. They were called Naasenes (a word possibly from Hebrew, nahash, snake.) They were a Christian Gnostic sect lumped together with Orphites. Of course my first instinct was to relate Orphites with Orpheus but it seems to come from the Greek 'ophis' which again means snake. Hippolytus used the term for what he considered were heretical speculations concerning the serpent of Genesis.

I have always thought the Genesis story funny where God appears to want to keep mankind a bit stupid while the snake turns up and encourages man to eat from the Tree of Knowledge. So I was surprised that these Orphites also considered the snake to be the good guy. They had a complex theory concerning the origin of mankind mentioning the power of light, Sophia and suggesting a good and bad God, something similar to the Cathars. But where their theory becomes relevant to us is when they deal with a section in the Old Testament about the attack by fiery serpents of the Israelites. During the Exodus from Egypt when the traveling was hard.

'The people grew impatient on the way; they spoke against God and against Moses, and said, "Why have you brought us up out of Egypt to die in the wilderness? There is no bread! There is no water! And we detest this miserable food!" Then the Lord sent fiery serpents among them; they bit the people and many Israelites died. The people came to Moses and said, "We sinned when we spoke against the Lord and against you. Pray that the Lord will take the serpents away from us." So Moses prayed for the people.

The Lord said to Moses, "Make a snake and put it up on a pole; anyone who is bitten can look at it and live." So Moses made a bronze snake and put it up on a pole. Then when anyone was bitten by a snake and looked at the bronze snake, they lived. (Numbers 21:4)

So God was punishing the Israelites for grumbling against himself and Moses by sending these serpents. But then God provides them with a remedy, the bronze serpent on a pole. If they look up to serpent he will save you.

Now not only do the Orphites make a big deal of this bronze serpent that held redemption for the moaning Israelites but in the Bible Jesus himself refers to the event when Nicodemus visits Him at night:

"Jesus said, "Very truly I tell you, no one can see the kingdom of God unless they are born again."

Jesus then explains about being born again.

Just as Moses lifted up the snake in the wilderness, so the Son of Man must be lifted up, that everyone who believes may have eternal life in him."(John 3:14)

Here is a Church interpretation of the saying – 'We are all under the condemnation of eternal death because of our sin. No human remedy can help. God graciously provided the way of salvation for us. He sent His own Son to be like that snake, lifted up in the wilderness.'

So the Orphites also considered the snake on the pole would offer eternal life to those who looked up to him. This I believe could be the actual reason behind the crucifixion ritual.

There is one other aspect of this that the Church proclaims - *so the Son of Man must be lifted up, that everyone who believes may have eternal life in him.*

This is supposed to be predicting Jesus' crucifixion. But suppose it was not a prediction but a statement of fact. Even those who have accepted the concept that the Crucifixion of Jesus may have been a ritual, assume it took place at the end of his ministry. But of course it would most likely to have occurred already, at the beginning.

You may be thinking that I have no real evidence to suggest the crucifixion occurred at the beginning of Jesus ministry, not the end, but let me show you a report by Eusebius who, when attacking a heretical group, makes a massive mistake.

"For the things that they have dared to say concerning the passion of the Savior are put into the fourth consulship of Tiberius, which occurred in the seventh year of his reign; at which time it is plain that Pilate was not yet ruling in Judea, if the testimony of Josephus is to be believed, who clearly shows in the above mentioned work (Antiquities) that Pilate was made Procurator of Judea by Tiberius in the twelfth year of his reign.' (Ecclesiastical History ch. 9 - Eusebius)

So what has he said that is so damning? He was attacking critics for having placed the crucifixion at a date that must be wrong because Pilate had not yet arrived in Israel. This one statement has been passed over by Biblical Scholars who believe that, if Jesus existed Pilate was involved with his death – so they think Eusebius' criticism is correct because how could anyone claim the crucifixion occurred before Pilate arrived in Judea? But of course the truth is that the ritual crucifixion *did* occur at the beginning of Jesus ministry before Pilate arrived in Judea, not at the end of his life. Look again:

"For the things that they have dared to say concerning the passion of the Savior are put into the fourth consulship of Tiberius, which occurred in the seventh year of his reign; at which time it is plain that Pilate was not yet ruling in Judea."

But this is not the only piece of evidence. A Gnostic document agrees with this assumption that the death and resurrection ritual occurred at the beginning.

'It came to pass, when Jesus had risen from the dead, that he passed eleven years discoursing with his disciples, and instructing them only up to the regions of the First Commandment and up to the regions of the First Mystery, that within the Veil, within the First Commandment, which is the four-and-twentieth mystery without and below.' (Pistis Sophia)

If he died in 38 AD then this event would have happened in the early twenties as part of the ritual that made him a full initiate before he undertook his mission. It could also have been the event that made him famous, as that seems to have happened to Lazarus after his resurrection/initiation.

'Meanwhile a large crowd of Jews found out that Jesus was there and came, not only because of him but also to see Lazarus, whom he had raised from the dead.' (John 12:9)

This could also explain why the family who live in Bethany are present at the crucifixion but none of the disciples are as they had not yet been employed.

'Near the cross of Jesus stood his mother, his mother's sister, Mary the wife of Clopas, and Mary Magdalene.' (John 19:25)

And he gives instructions to Lazarus as he moves out of normal existence to a higher level – which we will explain later.

'When Jesus saw his mother there, and the disciple whom he loved standing nearby, he said to her, "Woman, here is your son," and to the disciple, "Here is your mother." From that time on, this disciple took her into his home.' (John 19:26)

Chapter Twenty-three

INSIDE THE TOMB

'Joseph of Arimathea was accompanied by Nicodemus, the man who earlier had visited Jesus at night. Nicodemus brought a mixture of myrrh and aloes, about seventy-five pounds, they took the body of Jesus and bound it in linen wrappings.' ' (John 19:39)

Presumably there are funeral directors in ancient Israel, as the body is ritually unclean, so requires washing and having the hair and nails cut. But who carries out this process for Jesus? Two members of the Sanhedrin, who are secret associates of Jesus, function as funeral directors. Why would a couple of rich, bigwigs like Joseph of Arimathea and Nicodemus suddenly turn up with all the trappings of funeral directors to perform this unclean process? And remember how unclean dead bodies are:

'He shall not go near to a dead person... But if a man dies very suddenly beside him and he defiles his dedicated head of hair, then he shall shave his head and put it on the fire'
(Num. 6:1)

So like me you must be asking yourself, what were they actually doing in the tomb? The answer lies in the moment shown in hundreds of paintings called *Noli me tangere*.

Yes, it is the moment when Mary Magdalene finds the tomb empty and turns and sees someone who she mistakes for a gardener. Mistaking Jesus for a gardener in Jerusalem is strange enough in itself. It makes no sense to expect a gardener to be wandering around the site of execution, arranging the flowers. But a large house in Bethany that has a garden with a tomb in it, that makes sense. But what exactly is happening in these *Noli me tangere,* paintings?

Perhaps I can explain with a quote from Josephus about the initiation of the Essenes into higher degrees.

'They are divided into four classes, according to their duration in the training, and the later-joiners are so inferior to the earlier-joiners that if they should touch them, the latter wash themselves off as if they have mingled with a foreigner.' (Josephus)

What does *Noli me tangere* mean? Do not touch me! Why? Because he has been initiated to a higher level.

Interestingly, Priscillian, the very first supposed heretic killed by the Church of Rome in AD 385, distinguished three degrees of initiation, though he did not deny hope of pardon to those who were unable to attain full perfection.

'Noli me tangere' has no other logical explanation and the church even suggest Jesus says this because he has moved to a higher level. What higher level can it be other than a higher level of initiation, which is exactly what the original Christian Gnostics believed?

Chapter Twenty-four

IN THE TOMB

While I am pretty certain about what has unfolded so far, I am afraid I am going to introduce you to a crazy theory that I cannot confirm one way or the other, but there is some evidence for it.

Now the Bible tells us Joseph of Arimathea and Nicodemus attended to the body of Jesus in the tomb. And I asked the question, *what were two big-wigs doing in the tomb?'* And answered that they were performing a rite to take Jesus on to a higher level of initiation. In his book *Genisis: The First Book of Revelations*, David Wood makes an outlandish suggestion as to what that rite may have been, that has bugged me ever since I read it.

Wood claimed that the relics of Joseph were the cup that caught the Holy Blood, a sponge and a reed, and with these he suggests they removed Jesus phallus! I know this sounds really weird but genital mutilation is still a part of religions, especially the act of circumcision by the Jews. Castration was commonly performed on slaves to make them docile and even in Europe, on young male singers, to keep their voices high. The last Castrato died in 1922. Some eunuchs had both their testicles and phallus removed and a reed was used to keep the urethra open. It is not life threatening, as there have been hundreds of cases of women cutting off the organs of their unfaithful husbands. In fact, in the 1970s, in Thailand alone, over a hundred cases were recorded. There have also been many reports of the penis being reattached successfully.

David Wood quotes both the myth of Isis and Osiris and the story of the Fisher King to give credence to the theory. Osiris was killed by Seth and his body cut into fifteen pieces and scattered over the land of Egypt. Isis located fourteen parts of the body and using her magic fused them together. But she was missing the penis. She pleaded with Thoth, the Lord of Measures and he loaned her his measuring reed as a substitute phallus. From the union a son, Horus was born by this non-carnal union.

The Holy Grail story of the Fisher King tells how the King is injured in the groin and is therefore infertile. At a banquet a salver is brought in with a bleeding lance. Wood suggests that the Fisher King is Jesus (the fish) and concludes the bleeding lance is his phallus imitating the ceremony performed on Jesus by Nicodemus and Joseph of Arimathea in the tomb.

I find it as difficult to believe as you do but there is a strange parallel that Wood never quotes but which made me wonder if any of this could be true. It is the story of Abelard and Heloise, whose tomb can be found in Pere Lachaise cemetery in Paris.

Could their story be an attempt to parallel the Jesus and Magdalene story?

In twelfth century Paris, the intellectually gifted young Heloise, the niece of Fulbert, no less a person than the Canon of Notre Dame, strove for knowledge. The only teacher in Paris that could provide the education that she seeks is the famous philosopher, Peter Abelard, who is employed by the Canon to teach her. Though twenty years her senior, Abelard quickly becomes intrigued by Heloise's uncommon wit and intelligence. They soon find themselves so entwined that neither can resist the spiritual and physical desires of their bodies. Heloise becomes pregnant and the Canon in revenge cuts off Abelard's penis. He survived the attack and became an even more famous lecturer and philosopher.

Now the question is, was this an attack, or was the story told to conceal the real nature of the event? One of Abelard's letters states that the attack took place in a secret room in his house. Why would he have a secret room and if it was secret how do the attackers know about it? The second thing is that this event occurs around 1117, exactly the same time as the Knights Templars were formed. The reason why this could be important is that if the Templars were linked to the Jewish Royal families who escaped the disaster in Jerusalem and went to the south of France, as did Mary Magdalene. If anyone knew the truth about the events in the tomb it would be them.

It could all be just an odd coincidence and Abelard was attacked by the Canon of Notre Dame, who cut off his penis in a fit of spite, but is it likely?

If you think this is just too drastic for anyone to do, then let me quote to you from Eusebius writing about the Early Church father, Origen Adamantiu:

"While Origen was conducting catechetical instruction at Alexandria, a deed was done by him, which evidenced an immature and youthful mind, but at the same time gave the highest proof of faith and continence. For he took the words: 'There are eunuchs who have made themselves eunuchs for the kingdom of heaven's sake', (Matthew 19:12) in too literal and extreme a sense. And in order to fulfill the Savior's word, and at the same time to take away from the unbelievers all opportunity for scandal – for although young he met for the study of divine things with women as well as men – he carried out in action the word of the Savior." (Eusebius Pamphilus)

Love this picture although I am not sure what the Nuns are doing and is the man diving into the fires of Hell?

So Origen who understood the nature of Jesus, seems to have cut off his penis, and strangely after this event, just like Peter Abelard, he became *'great and distinguished among all men...his fame increased greatly....being known for virtue and wisdom.'*

But why would this total castration be considered a move to a higher level of initiation? Perhaps it involves the concept of a pure human, neither male nor female. To understand this fully we must look to those initiated to the highest level amongst the Cathars, the true descendants of the Jesus religion. They believed that, after initiation, the Holy Spirit was able to descend and dwell within the body of the new Priest, (or Perfect which is what they called their Priests) hence the austere lifestyle needed to provide a pure dwelling place for the Spirit. Once in this state of housing the Holy Spirit within themselves, the Perfect was thought to have become 'trans-material or semi-angelic, not yet released from the confines of the body but containing within them an enhanced spirituality which linked them to God. As an angel is neither man nor woman, is this the higher level Jesus aspired to? And is this the inside knowledge that the Magdalene taught to the people of the Languedoc? I should mention that the highest Cathar priests were celibate but I can't tell you if this was by will power or by fact.

The one question we have to ask is, if this amputation took place, did Jesus and the Magdalene have sex before the operation as Abalard and Heloise did? And like Heloise, did Magdalene become pregnant and have a baby? Certainly a lot of people have argued that such a baby existed, especially after both the fiction book, *'Da Vinci Code'* and the non-fiction *'Holy Blood Holy Grail'* claimed the Holy Grail *(French - Sang Graal)* was in fact the blood royal child of Jesus and Mary from which a holy blood line was produced. Even though the writers of 'Holy Blood' make a reason case for such an idea they had to admit that in the end it was just speculation. But the 'Da Vinci Code' convinced a lot of people it was true.

The amputation could explain one event that has puzzled me, that is why the Magdalene cried tears when she anointed Jesus feet and wiped them with her hair. Did she cry for the sacrifice of the sexuality of her loved one?

I cannot say if any of this is true but it turned up in my investigation and I leave it for your consideration. For the last word on the subject, and so you won't consider me a total crank for suggesting these possibilities, let me quote you Jesus' words from Matthew 19:12.

'For there are eunuchs who have been so from birth, and there are eunuchs who have been made eunuchs by men, and there are eunuchs who have made themselves eunuchs for the sake of the kingdom of heaven. Let the one who is able to receive this, receive it." (Matthew 19:12)

Are you able to receive this information or is it all just far too shocking? It certainly makes me wonder if this is true.

Chapter Twenty-five

THE NATIVITY

Once I had unraveled the Jesus story other things fell into place. Understanding the Holy Grail stories and why Joseph of Arimathea is often mentioned in them, or who was behind the formation of the Templars. Another thing that unfolded was who was the second Judas at the last Supper.

'When Judas had taken the bread, he went out. And it was night.' (John 13:30)

Which is followed by:

'Judas (not Iscariot) said to him, "Lord, how is it that you will reveal yourself to us?" (John 14:22)

Two Judases, but only one is listed in Matthew:

'The first, Simon, who is called Peter, and Andrew his brother; and James the son of Zebedee, and John his brother; Philip and Bartholomew; Thomas and Matthew the tax collector; James the son of Alphaeus, and Thaddaeus; Simon the Zealot, and Judas Iscariot, the one who betrayed Him.' (Matthew 10:2)

Only one Judas is named, the one who betrays him so who is this second Judas?

Besides the Gospels, the only modern reference I can find that might refer to the second Judas are these two statues on either side of the altar in the heretical church at Rennes-le-Château.

Astrology was an important part of ancient belief systems and of course a star is mentioned at the birth of Jesus and while you cannot follow a star for directions to a stable or even a palace, it is important because of a Star Prophecy that was well known.

"There shall come a star out of Jacob" (Numbers 24:17)
In 11 BC Halley's comet appeared in the sky and certainly anyone born under its light could well be considered auspicious. Mind you, there is one other astronomical event that I consider more likely. It is placed by writers Knight and Lomas on the 25th December, 7 BC, rising twenty-two minutes before the sun, a conjunction between Venus and Mercury which would have caused a striking bright star appearing just before dawn for about half an hour, when looking from Jerusalem towards the Mount of Olives. The forty-year Venus cycle figures prominently in the Bible and it is suggested the Holy of Holies had a high window, which would allow magical light from Venus as the morning star, to fall on to the Ark of the Covenant. Josephus reports an

especially bright occurrence appearing at exactly that time - just before sunrise.

'At the ninth hour of the night, so great a light shone around the altar and the Temple, that it appeared to be the brightness of midday. This light continued for half an hour... and was interpreted by the sacred Scribes as a portent of events that immediately followed upon it. (Josephus, War)

I leave it to you to decide if any of these astronomical sightings have any significance to our story but one of the most important of astrological events was occurring around the time of Jesus birth.

The earth spins as it goes round the sun. It also has a wobble. Imagine a spinning top, the central axis is not perfectly upright, it inscribes a slight circle which gets bigger as the top slows, till it falls. A full circle of the top's wobble takes a fraction of a second. The earth's wobble takes some twenty six thousand years to make one circle. This is called the Platonic year after Plato who was initiated into this information during his years of study in Egypt. Obviously the ancients did not know about the wobble, what they saw was the rising sun changing its position in relation to background stars. Every two thousand years it moved from one constellation to another and therefore became known as 'the precession of the equinoxes'.

Ten thousand years ago the sun rose in the constellation of Leo, that is why some people believe that the Sphinx, which points to Leo, was built then. Eight thousand years ago it moved into the sign of Taurus, so the Bull became a sacred symbol for the ancient Egyptians. Two thousand years after that, the sun moved into Aries, the ram. At that time Alexander the Great conquered Egypt and was initiated into this knowledge by the priests at Memphis. He then portrayed himself on coins, with ram's horns as the chosen one of his age.

Incidentally this is the meaning of the song 'The dawning of the age of Aquarius' from the musical 'Hair' which indicates the latest movement of the rising sun into the water sign, Aquarius? Around the time of the birth of Christ, the sun was moving into the constellation of Pisces. As the chosen one of this new age, Christians equated Jesus with Pisces the fish and therefore used the fish as the symbol for him. The astrological sign for Pisces, is never shown as a single fish, but always represented as two fish.

And the only other Zodiacal sign that has a double image and sits opposite Pisces in the Zodiac circle is Gemini, the twins!. Because of the movement of the sun into Pisces there was an expectation of the birth of twins amongst mystics especially if the birth was accompanied by another astronomical event like the conjunction between Venus and Mercury, that would make the twins very important.

Okay, you obviously think that any suggestion I might make that Jesus had a twin brother is ridiculous and that there is no evidence for such an idea. But strangely there is such evidence and the idea that Jesus had a twin, was one of the most persistent and tenacious of the ancient heresies.

In the Bible, a disciple is called Thomas. Thomas is not a name it is the Aramaic word for twin, similar to the Hebrew, which clearly suggests he is somebody's twin. And if you doubt that Thomas means twin in Aramaic, then in the Bible he is sometimes called Thomas Didymus. But weirdly Didymus is a Greek word which is also the word for twin. So this Mr. Twin Twin, definitely suggests there was a twin amongst Jesus' entourage and there is a clear attempt to conceal his real name. To believe in the idea of a twin, first we would need evidence that Jesus had a brother. Well, in the Bible it clearly says in the original book of Mark:

"Isn't this Mary's son and the brother of James, Joseph, Judas and Simon? Aren't his sisters here with us?" (Mark 6:3)

These brothers are also mentioned in Matthew 13:55. So he definitely had brothers and sisters, which makes the Roman Church's pronouncement that Mary died and went to heaven still intact, some trick! The Church attempts to wriggle out of the Biblical evidence by saying things like 'they were Joseph's sons of a previous marriage', or 'Jesus considered everybody especially the Disciples as brothers'. But the Biblical statements don't say that; and in fact Acts of the Apostles states quite clearly:

'Those present were Peter, John, James and Andrew; Philip and Thomas, Bartholomew and Matthew; James son of

Alphaeus and Simon the Zealot, and Judas son of James. They all joined together constantly in prayer, along with the women and Mary the mother of Jesus, and with his brothers.' (Acts 1:13)

Jesus' brother James became the leader of the group after Jesus' death and Paul calls him '*The brother of the Lord.*'

Well the texts where Jesus was clearly mentioned to have a twin were in general use, till the Bible was formulated by Rome and all other texts were destroyed. Except in the case of certain Egyptian Monks, who felt unable to destroy their Holy texts, so hid them in jars in the desert at Nag Hammadi where they were discovered in 1945. One of these non-canonical gospels, is the *Gospel of Thomas* which states:

'These are the secret sayings that the living Jesus spoke and Didymus Judas Thomas recorded.'

Furthermore from *Acts of Thomas* we have:

'Twin brother of Christ, apostle of the Most High and fellow initiate into the hidden word of Christ, who does receive his secret sayings.'

So not only is Judas the real name of Thomas but this actually states he is Jesus twin. There is even an incantation:

Come Holy Spirit... Holy Dove that bearest the twin young. Come, Hidden Mother...'

So Judas is the hidden name in the Bible of Thomas, and it was accidentally left in the Last Supper for us to discover. It does suggest there was an actual real event the Gospel was reporting on, which has been cut and added to, to conform to the Roman Church's version of Jesus. But they slipped up big-time to have left this in.

If you want confirmation from the Academic world, from someone who can read the original texts in Hebrew and Aramaic, let me quote from Prof. Robert Eisenman one of the most respected researchers in the ancient history of Israel.

'The claim implicit in the name 'Judas Thomas, is that he is a twin, 'thoma' in Aramaic meaning twin. The implication usually is that he is a twin of Jesus, his third brother'

Surprisingly Professor Eisenman is not alone in the Academic world to have presented the idea that Jesus had a twin, so why is it such a shock to people. In 1931 Dr. Robert Eisler published a paper called, *'The Messiah Jesus and John the Baptist. According to Flavius Josephus and other Jewish and Christian Sources.* This was not some obscure document because Eisler with his knowledge of all the ancient languages was able to filter documents of interpolations to identify the appearance of Jesus. So one would expect his Chapter *Ecce Homo* sub section *The Early tradition about a twin brother and double of Jesus',* would be equally well known. But somehow the information has not been allowed to become common knowledge even though it states:

The parallel passages in the 'Acts of Thomas' where time and again Judah Thauma, i.e. 'Judas the Twin' appears as strikingly like his deceased brother, whose twin he was.'

Furthermore after quoting many sources, Eisler reasons

'There can be no question about the essential fact that a tradition like this does not spring up overnight and without historical foundation of some sort. For what Christian would

have been foolish enough to invent such a legend, seeing that it is most apt to undermine the very basis of orthodox tradition' (Dr. Eisler).

In the ancient Safed Scroll, discovered near Lake Tiberius in 1882, whether it is real or fake, it again states there were two brothers called Yeshua and Judas, who were the illegitimate twin sons born of a fifteen-year-old girl. I can't tell you whether this text is a forgery or not, but what it does tell us is that even in 1882 someone believed in the idea of twins and produced this document. Or perhaps this is a genuine scroll and there were twins called Yeshua and Judas at the time.

The two most telling moments in the Bible that seem to confirm the twin idea is firstly the attempt to conceal Thomas' real name, Judas, but then it has accidentally been left in at the Last Supper. But more importantly, the first moment Jesus appears after the crucifixion, there are two parallel verses one without specifying Thomas presence and the next emphasizing it. Is this to counteract the probable criticism that Jesus did not resurrect; it was just his twin appearing?

'So when it was evening on the first day of the week, and when the doors were shut where the disciples were, for fear of the Jews, Jesus came and stood in their midst and said to them, "Peace be with you." He showed them both His hands and His side. The disciples then rejoiced. So Jesus said to them again, "Peace be with you."

Did someone then raise the issue of the twin because the scene is then repeated, exactly the same, but now with Thomas clearly present to do a bit of *doubting*.

'After eight days His disciples were again inside, and Thomas

with them. Jesus came, the doors having been shut, and stood in their midst and said, "Peace be with you." Then He said to Thomas, "Reach here with your finger, and see my hands."(John 20:19)

There you go, the same scene, with the doors again closed and with Jesus being boringly repetitive with his *"Peace be with you."* But this time emphasizing that Thomas Didymus; Mr. Twin Twin, was there. There is no logical reason for the scene to be repeated word for word, except to add that Thomas was definitely present to counteract any critic who complained it was the twin appearing, not the resurrected Jesus. The early critic Celsus states that every time he raises an argument, the Christians add sections even to their own Holy books. We know this particular section is a forgery because several of the insertions into John are late on when they were trying to separate Jesus from the Jews so the texts have:

'When the doors were shut where the disciples were, for fear of the Jews.'

This is a typically ludicrous insertion because Jesus and the disciples are obviously Jews too. So the story of doubting Thomas must be a late insertion.

The twin idea was a strong belief of Priscillian, the fourth-century teacher, who was Bishop of Avila. He treated women as equals; he celebrated the Sabbath on Saturday and clearly followed Jesus' Jewish roots. One of his dedicated disciples, a woman named Egeria, journeyed in 381 to the Middle East to seek out un-canonical texts. She visited Edessa the centre of Thomasine teaching. Edessa is now Urfa in modern Turkey, which had long been the centre of the twin cult of Momim and Aziz. This pair had been supplanted by Jesus and Judas Thomas. Perhaps it was through Egeria returning with the texts, that Priscillian believed that Jesus had a twin. But then in AD 386, Priscillian became the first heretic to be executed by the Church of Rome. So have you any wonder that believing in the twin idea slowly slipped underground till it has been forgotten.

Well not quite totally forgotten, because in the Templar stronghold in the Languedoc, a priest in that mysterious church of Rennes-le-Château dealt with in the book 'Holy Blood and Holy Grail', has a very nice pair of statues facing each other in pride of place either side of the altar. They are Mary with one baby Jesus in her arms and Joseph with the other.

The dawning of the age of Pisces. That is certainly one of the secret mysteries that the church of Rennes-le-Château contains, and presumably known among all Cathars of the region and perhaps the Knights Templar.

I did suggest this is the only reference I could find of the twin idea, but there is one possible other. It is in the Magdalene church in Alicante. On either side of the tower are platforms for statues. One has Joseph with baby Jesus but the other has nothing! Was Mary with the other baby here before, or was it never completed for obvious reasons.

Chapter Twenty-six

JOHN THE BAPTIST

This chapter is not about things I know, they are things I don't know, but hope someone out there can complete the picture. One person who figures greatly in the Languedoc and in esoteric circles is John the Baptist who has many churches dedicated to him in the area. According to the Bible, the Baptist was born a few months before Jesus and was related to him. Also Jesus is said to have been baptized by John and then after John's death, Jesus begins his ministry. For some reason the Templars and esoteric circles in France seem to believe John was more important than Jesus. I cannot find why but looking at the statue of the Baptist in the church of Rennes-le-Château it certainly seems true.

There are hundreds of books about how the Priest, Abbé Saunière suddenly became rich and with this inexplicable money carried out major works on the church. And vital to us is that he inserted heretical information in many of the stained-glass windows and statues he erected.

Can you see that Saunière's statue of the Baptist appears to show the Baptist as the more important person, with Jesus being very deferential? The Baptist's costume even gives him more stature than the usual accepted Baptist's dress. If you don't see it, compare it to a more typical statue of the Baptism.

I will show you that this is not an accident, there is a definite belief in the area that the Baptist was more important than Jesus.

What about that other esoteric church St. Sulpice in Paris, which has been a hotbed for both occultism and modernism and mentioned for its links to occult knowledge in the books, Holy Blood and the Da Vinci Code? Much is talked about weird details inside, but for some reason nobody mentions what is outside. Round to the right side of the church, there imposingly built into a niche, is a huge statue of John the Baptist. Why do both these churches, known for their heretical content, portray the Baptist so prominently when they are not churches dedicated to the Baptist?

What do you make of the pointing finger? Either it points to heaven, which could be a feature of any religious statue, or perhaps like the statue in Rennes-le-Château it is a statue proclaiming that John the Baptist is number one!

Okay you think this is a bit far-fetched? But consider the pointing finger in Leonardo's paintings of the Virgin of the Rocks. There are two, one in the Paris Louvre and the other in London.

In the Louvre version, the angel is pointing at one of the babies, but is it Jesus or John? A later artist added a reed cross to the London version suggesting the baby the Angel in the Louvre is pointing at is the Baptist. He is placed higher than Jesus who looks up at him. Was the Louvre version painted first and the church demanded the finger to be removed because it suggested John is more important than Jesus?

You don't buy that one either do you? I would agree with you if that was the only pointing finger we have to consider. But now we come to the more mischievous finger pointing by Leonardo?

This, would you believe, is a painting by Leonardo of John the Baptist. If you were not told, there is no way you would think it was John with that weird, knowing smile. Do you believe what the National Gallery says about the finger?

'The finger pointing to heaven, alludes to Christ's future destiny'.

Surely not! With that knowing grin he is supposed to be thinking of Jesus' death and resurrection? Come on, this clearly has absolutely nothing to do with Christ's passion.

Leonardo is clearly trying to tell us something. Remember some academics have claimed that Leonardo was a Rosicrucian or at least had, what they call, Rosicrucian beliefs.

I accept that this is all hard to accept. I need then to introduce you to another pointing finger in Leonardo's 'The Burlington House Cartoon'. You've probably never noticed that the design appears perfect, but then hardly visible is the finger pointing upwards. Do you see it, upper right?

Here is the National Gallery description:

'The Virgin Mary sits on the lap of her mother, Saint Anne. The Christ Child blesses his cousin Saint John the Baptist. Leonardo also treated the meeting of the two children in his

Surely that older woman is not Mary's mother, Ann. The older woman has to be, Elizabeth the mother of John the Baptists who was said to be too old to have children. But the finger! No mention of the finger indicating what?

I imagine you are beginning to think that maybe I am not so crazy after all, and there is something going on with these fingers. So perhaps you should look at Leonardo's painting of the Last Supper. Look at the disciple thrusting the index finger up into Jesus' face. The finger is framed against black so it is meant to stand out.

So much has been talked about this painting but nobody ever mentions the finger, which he appears to be thrusting into Jesus' face. Is it to say someone else is number one?

Strangely, Freemasons also seem to hold the Baptist in high esteem. Here is a statement from one Masonic Lodge on a pamphlet declaring the most important day of the Freemason's year:

'By history, custom, tradition and ritualistic requirements, the Craft holds in veneration the Festival Day of St. John the Baptist on June 24th.

The document continues to admit:

"No satisfactory explanation has yet been advanced to explain why."

But it is clear from a painting in the same document that, like the statue in Rennes-le-Château that someone is placing John above Jesus.

The whole thing raises several questions. Clearly the Masons writing this document don't know why they are celebrating John the Baptist. So does this remind us of Eliphas Levi's comment:

'The Chiefs alone knew whither they were going; the rest followed unsuspectingly.'

This was a comment about the Templars but can it also be true of the Freemasons, and that both organizations had secret chiefs who set the agenda? Or is it just that the agenda was set years ago and the motives have since been forgotten?

Let me tell you about a collection of documents, deposited anonymously in the Bibliothèque Nationale in Paris during the 1960s. They contain rather odd but accurate information about French history concerning the Church at Rennes-le-Château and certain underground organizations including the Templars. All were written under pseudonyms or attributed to people later found to be deceased and who, as far as researchers could tell, had nothing to do with them. One of the authors was finally discovered to be Philippe de Chéresey and was said by him to be a sort of surrealist joke to create a supposedly ancient organization called the Priory of Sion. This Priory of Sion, in fact was not ancient as it was first registered in 1956. So now the whole event is taken as a hoax. The problem is that some of the information is so obscure yet so accurate that it would take years of research to discover – just for a joke?

I am not saying Philippe de Chéresey's dossiers were not a hoax, I am saying that they had a source of information not available to the Academic world and they used it to give credence to their 'so called' joke. We will deal with this unnamed source later but the dossiers list an unbelievable list of Grand Masters from a splinter group of the Templars. I cannot tell you if it is real, but I cannot quite believe anyone could write a list of 26 people, which starts in 1188 to recent times, which links known and little-known people whose interconnections actually are not obvious, without a great deal of research. It would be a massive undertaking just for a gag.

It is said the people in the list were not called Grand Masters but Nautonniers, which is French for Navigators. So here is the extraordinary, or perhaps ridiculous, list of Nautonniers.

Jean de Gisors (1188–1220)
Marie de Saint-Clair (1220–1266)-
Guillaume de Gisors (1266–1307)
Edouard de Bar (1307–1336)
Jeanne de Bar (1336–1351)
Jean de Saint-Clair (1351–1366)
Blanche d'Évreux (1366–1398)
Nicolas Flamel (1398–1418)
René d'Anjou (1418–1480)
Iolande de Bar (1480–1483)
Sandro Botticelli (1483–1510)
Leonardo da Vinci (1510–1519)
Connétable de Bourbon (1519–1527)
Ferrante I Gonzaga (1527–1575)
Ludovico Gonzaga (1575–1595)
Robert Fludd (1595–1637)
J. Valentin Andrea (1637–1654)
Robert Boyle (1654–1691)
Isaac Newton (1691–1727)
Charles Radclyffe (1727–1746)
Charles de Lorraine (1746–1780)
Maximilian de Lorraine (1780–1801)
Charles Nodier (1801–1844)
Victor Hugo (1844–1885)
Claude Debussy (1885–1918)
Jean Cocteau (1918–1963)

In 1629 a man named Robert Denyau, curé of Gisors, composed a history of the Gisors family, the *'Histoire polytique de Gisors et du pays de Vulcsain.'* This manuscript now in the Bibliotèque de Rouen states that the Rose-Croix was founded by the first on the list, Jean de Gisors. So this suggests the list is a list of members of l'Ordre de la Rose-Croix Veritas not the Priory of Sion.

Originally the Rosicrucian organization was thought to be founded by a Christian Rosenkreutz who wrote the Rosicrucian manifesto, *The Chemical Wedding*, but it was later admitted that this was written by a member of the above list, Johann Valentin Andrea, a German theologian who confessed he had written it as a 'ludibrium'- a joke! Not another joke?

Anyway true or fake, these Chiefs all take on the name John and a number (John XXI followed by John XXII) But what is interesting is that the first, Jean de Gisors is John II. The writers of the "Holy Blood, Holy Grail" who first published the list, were unsure which historical John was John I, but they suspected it was John the Baptist. Can we now be certain that John I was John the Baptist, which explains the raised index finger in the paintings, telling us who exactly was number one?

You still don't believe me? Look again at the painting. The right hand index finger indicates one, but look who his other hand is pointing to. His left hand points to himself!

There can be no doubt the Baptist is telling us *"I am number one"*.

When I first showed you the Baptist outside St. Sulpice with a finger raised and suggested it might indicate that he is number one, you probably thought I was bonkers, but now it is getting harder and harder to deny this possibility.

So if John the Baptist is number one then does this make Leonardo da Vinci, who was Nautonnier between 1510 to 1519, John XIII? And is that why he is selling in his paintings, his predecessor John the Baptist, as number one?

Furthermore the Priory of Sion is not an ancient organization, but did those trying to create it, use information from a source not available to Academics. Some documents had the name of Grand Lodge Alpina from Switzerland and there certainly is a link between the demise of the Templars and the formation of Switzerland, which carries the reversed Templar cross on its flag.

As the two books that mention the list of Nautonniers and the Priory of Sion, 'Holy Blood', and 'Da Vinci Code', have had such an influence and caused such argument about whether such an occult organization existed and whether Leonardo was part of it, I want to quote from a book written in 1978, well before the two books were written. The book is called 'The Hidden Art' and the author,

F. Gettings wrote about occult imagery in Leonardo paintings.

'One may only speculate where Leonardo obtained his knowledge of this heretical tradition, which we nowadays relate to 'esoteric Christianity', but which even in the sixteenth century would have been quite heretical....Perhaps Leonardo da Vinci was himself an initiate, a secret adept, and had the knowledge and had the insights from his own personal insights.'

 So art historian, Gettings had spotted something without any knowledge of the fake Priory of Sion story of the two later books, which does suggest something strange was going on in Leonardo's work.

I should show you another painting in the French church in central London, Notre Dame de France. It is by the last Nautonnier mentioned in the list, John Cocteau.

It is distinctly odd with its black sun. But what I find interesting is the rose on the cross, suggesting l'Ordre de la Rose-Croix Veritas. And the two grieving women, Mary Magdalene and Mary the mother, are curiously visually joined. Is that significant or am I reading something into this that is not there.

You may now be wondering why John the Baptist was considered, by some significant people, to be more important than Jesus? But I am afraid I don't know the answer to that, although I have a few vague theories

I hope you don't consider this to have been a waste of time, even if I cannot answer the basic question posed by this strange journey into Leonardo paintings. But the question it raises for me is, why do the people influenced by the Magdalene and Lazarus in the South of France consider the Baptist more important than Jesus. Is it something the Bethany family believed, and did they have a direct relationship to the Baptist? I hope someone reads this and solves the conundrum.

Chapter Twenty-seven

THE TWO HIGH PRIESTS

Let us recap on the contradictions that started unraveling the Jesus story. Remember biblical expert, Professor Robert Eisenman, wrote:

'A great deal of trouble is taken by these writers to get Jesus to Galilee.'(Robert Eisenman, Jesus and the Dead Sea Scrolls)

Without knowing our reasoning, the Professor had exposed the clear attempt to mix Jesus up with the Galilean and calling him Jesus of Nazareth, was obviously part of this process.

Secondly we suggest that Jesus was arrested by a crowd with Temple guards while it was Judas the Galilean's army that was attacked by the Cohort of Roman soldiers who killed his followers and arrested him.

Thirdly we exposed the contradiction that after the arrest, in the synoptic Gospels, Jesus is taken to High Priest Caiaphas, who was never High Priest and in the other Gospel he is taken to High Priest Annas who also was not High Priest at that time as he relinquished the post in AD 15. But we claimed that it was Annas who was in fact the High Priest who dealt with the trial of Jesus before the Sanhedrin because of the statement in Acts.

'The next day the rulers, the elders and the teachers of the law met in Jerusalem. Annas the High Priest was there, and so were Caiaphas, John, Alexander and others.' (Acts 4:6)

So Annas is clearly stated to be the High Priest at this time, whereas Caiaphas is just present (or inserted later). This is reinforced by the opening of Luke:

In the fifteenth year of the reign of Tiberius Caesar, Pontius Pilate being governor of Judea, and Herod being tetrarch of Galilee... during the High Priesthood of Annas and Caiaphas, the word of God came to John the son of Zechariah in the wilderness.' (Luke3:1)

Again the title is given to Annas while Caiaphas seems to be added as an after-thought. Surely if Annas is just an old man why state him first. I think we can be pretty certain that Annas is the real High Priest. But how can I claim he was involved with Jesus in AD 38 when he was High Priest only from AD 6 to AD 15?

Let me repeat all this again because it is of paramount importance. After the arrest, in the synoptic Gospels, Jesus is taken to High Priest Caiaphas, who was never High Priest, it was his son Joseph, while in John's Gospel Jesus was taken to High Priest Annas who also was not High Priest at that time as he relinquished the post in AD 15.

I am suggesting it was Joseph ben Caiaphas who was the High Priest who handed Judas the Galilean over to Pilate in AD 32 to save Roman reprisals:

'Caiaphas, who was high priest that year, said to them, "You know nothing at all, nor do you take into account that it is expedient for you that one man die for the people, and that the whole nation not perish". (John 11:49)

Handing over Judas the Galilean could save the Nation but this would not be true of handing over Jesus. Then I suggested it was Annas who was the High Priest who dealt with Jesus because of the statement in Acts.

'The next day the rulers, the elders and the teachers of the law met in Jerusalem. Annas the High Priest was there, and so were Caiaphas, John, Alexander and others.' (Acts 4:6)

But as yet I have not explained why I suggest Annas was the High Priest who was involved with Jesus in AD 38 when he was High Priest only from AD 6 to AD 15?

I have also not explained why they changed High Priest Joseph to High Priest Caiaphas, the name of his father? Even doctoring Josephus who would know very well that Caiaphas was never High Priest as his well-connected parents would probably personally know Caiaphas and his son Joseph. Yet he was supposed to have written:

'Caiaphas became a high priest during a turbulent period.' (Josephus Antiquities)

Surely this was originally:

*'**Joseph** became a high priest during a turbulent period.' (Josephus Antiquities)*

And why was it suggested that there were two High Priests?

During the high priesthood of Annas and Caiaphas, the word of God came to John son of Zechariah in the wilderness. (Luke 3:2)

Which then forced the church to try to explain this obvious error with their story that Annas was not the High Priest he was just a very influential retired High Priest? What possible reason could there be for bothering with all this weird manipulation? What are they trying to hide?

There is only one explanation that makes sense of all this mess but only if the timeline in this book is correct and Jesus died in 38 AD. There is no other possible explanation and it reveals the depths the Roman church went to, to conceal the true story of Jesus. Here it is.

The High Priest who took over after Joseph ben Caiaphas in AD 36 was Jonathan ben Annas, one of Annas' sons. High Priest Jonathan was followed in 37 AD, by his brother, Theophilus ben Annas. Now if the Church has used Joseph ben Caiaphas' father's name as his real name, Caiaphas; then have they done the same for Theophilus ben Annas and called him High Priest Annas who in AD 38 found Jesus guilty of blasphemy?

I could not believe it, but the sly buggers have used father's names for both of them to confuse and conceal the true dates. So the use of the name Caiaphas instead of Joseph is only done to be able to similarly use Annas instead of the very revealing Theophilus. What they did was cut the first part of each name to leave High Priest ~~Joseph ben~~ Caiaphas and High Priest ~~Theophilus ben~~ Annas.

So it is High Priest Theophilus ben Annas, who interviews Jesus after his arrest by the Temple guards, found him guilty of blasphemy and according to Jewish custom, had him stoned to death? His body would then be hung on a tree and buried before sunset. And clearly the Roman Governor at the time, Marullas, had nothing at all to do with this act of punishment for blasphemy.

Look in John how abrupt the editing is:

'Arrested Jesus and bound him, and led him to Annas first.

Surely not. This is how it must have read originally:

'Arrested Jesus and bound him, and led him to High Priest Theophilus ben Annas. (John 18)

This is also why Theophilus in his Annas form is confirmed as the High Priest at the interview with Peter after Jesus death. Here is the cut they made

'The teachers of the law met in Jerusalem. ~~*Theophilus ben*~~ *Annas the high priest was there.' (Acts 4:6)*

This also explains why Annas is first in Luke's statement.

During the high priesthood of Annas and Caiaphas, the word of God came to John son of Zechariah in the wilderness. (Luke 3:2)

There is no other explanation for this strange set of Biblical statements about the High Priests other than it was an attempt to conceal the facts this book has presented. And I think I have the right now to call them facts since there is absolutely no other possible explanation for these High Priest manipulations.

Chapter Twenty-eight

THE FINAL NAIL

Now for the final proof that the staking by Pilate is of Judas the Galilean not Jesus. Let us start with the fact that Judas the Galilean's second in command is a Zadok who probably anointed him as the King. Remember how Josephus described the Galilean's son's entry into Jerusalem:

'... in pomp to worship, decked with kingly robes and followed by a train of armed zealots.' (Josephus, War)

And add to this Judas's attitude to Roman tax.

'Judas said that this taxation was no better than an introduction to slavery, and exhorted the nation to assert their liberty.' (Josephus Antiquities)

So Judas has a claim to be king and refuses to pay tax. Compare this to Jesus' response when some want to make him King:

'Jesus, knowing that they intended to come and make him king by force, withdrew again to a mountain by himself. (John 6:15)

And we know Jesus' attitude to paying Roman tax:

"Show me the coin used for the tax." So they brought him a denarius. Jesus said to them, "Whose image is this, and whose inscription?" They replied, "Caesar's." He said to them, " Then

give to Caesar the things that are Caesar's, and to God the things that are God's". (Matthew 22:18)

And remember this:

'Then Levi held a great banquet for Jesus at his house, and a large crowd of tax collectors and others were eating with them.' (Luke 5:29)

When you look at Luke 23 it certainly appears that Pilate is interrogating the Galilean.

'Then the whole body of them got up and brought him before Pilate. And they began to accuse him, saying, "We found this man misleading our nation and forbidding to pay taxes to Caesar, and saying that he himself is Christ, a King." So Pilate asked him, saying, "Are You the King of the Jews?" And he answered him and said, "It is as you say". (Luke 23)

Why ask him if he is king of the Jews; why say he is against paying Roman taxes, which he is not. But why not ask him the real questions that relate to his activities. "Show us a miracle?" Or some other activity he was famous for? No, this man, whoever he is, is accused of refusing to pay Roman taxes, and making a claim to be a King of the Jews. This man is obviously not Jesus, who sits down to dinner with tax collectors and actually makes no claim to be king. Who else could it be other than Judas the Galilean who is more likely to stab the tax collector with his knife than stab his chicken pie.

In Mark, not only does Pilate ask if he is king of the Jews, but the soldiers then dress Jesus up as a king to ridicule him. Why? It makes no sense whatsoever if nowhere in Mark's Gospel has he claimed to be a king. And in fact it actually makes the soldiers look really stupid not Jesus. But it does make perfect sense if this insertion is about Judas the Galilean being ridiculed by the soldiers. The whole Pilate story is totally discredited by the fact that Pilate's accusations of kingship and tax evasion do not follow the previous text in any shape or form. This is so obvious that some academics have drawn the wrong conclusion, writing that Jesus was a rebel against the Roman Empire and his revolutionary activities have been cut from the Gospels.

In fact, if the High Priest wants Jesus killed and one supposes, for argument sake, that he cannot stone him for blasphemy, where would he take Jesus to get him killed for claiming to be the King? Not to the Romans at all! But obviously to the actual king who Jesus is attempting to oust, none other than King Herod who we are told is in Jerusalem for Passover. Herod would soon chop his head off as he did to the Baptist for threatening his legitimacy. The logic of this is shown in Matthew's nativity story, the other place where baby Jesus is claimed to be King of the Jews by the Magi. Here King Herod's father, Herod the Great, logically goes all out to get this baby Jesus killed. Even if this is a totally fake story, it has an undeniable logic. But here in the crucifixion story, Jesus is actually sent by Pilate to King Herod, who, you assume would immediately chop his head off for trying to usurp his throne? But no, instead he asks Jesus to show off his special powers. Didn't they tell him Jesus was usurping his throne?

'The chief priests and the teachers of the law were standing there, vehemently accusing him. Then Herod and his soldiers ridiculed and mocked him. Dressing him in an elegant robe, they sent him back to Pilate.' (Luke 23:10)

Come on, chop his head off don't send him back to Pilate dressed as a king, especially as Pilate is obviously reluctant to kill him. What an utter mess! They have now dressed him up twice as a king! As a great man once said, *'Oh what a tangled web we weave, when first we practice to deceive.'*

There are a couple of things I am baffled by. One is why academics buy into the ridiculous idea that High Priest Joseph was actually called High Priest Caiaphas, the name of his father? It is clearly nonsense, no High Priest in the history of Israel has ever been called by his father's name, it is bonkers, and as stated, it is like calling John the Baptist, Zechariah the Baptist. Has everyone gone bananas to accept this utter tosh? There can only be one logical reason and that is by using the father's name for High Priest Joseph they can legitimately use the father's name for High Priest Theophilus, as using his real name would give away the date of his tenure which was from AD 37 to 41. This is absolutely confirmed that Theophilus was the High Priest when in Acts under the name High Priest Annas he deals with Peter.

The other odd thing that seems to be accepted by academics but is clearly nonsense is, the statement in John that the Sanhedrin are not allowed to stone Jews for blasphemy. Why would anyone accept that as true when people are being stoned left right and centre.

One thing I think needs to be explored is why the expert on the Roman Empire, Edward Gibbon, was so sure that those who were blamed by Nero for the Great Fire of Rome were the followers of Judas the Galilean, not the Christians.

'Although the genuine followers of Moses [Jews] were innocent of the fire of Rome, there had arisen among them a new and pernicious sect of Galileans, which was capable of the most horrid crimes... The followers of Judas, who impelled their countrymen into rebellion, were soon buried under the

ruins of Jerusalem, whilst those of Jesus, known by the more celebrated name of Christians, diffused themselves over the Roman Empire. How natural was it for Tacitus, in the time of Hadrian, to appropriate to the Christians the guilt and the sufferings, which he might, with far greater truth and justice, have attributed to a sect whose odious memory was almost extinguished.' (Gibbon: The Decline and Fall)

Combined with Tacitus statement this is virtually saying Pilate killed Judas the Galilean. How did he come to this conclusion? He did not do it the same way I did. And the forging of the 'e' into an 'i' in Chrestos had not yet been discovered. He must have seen a document or maybe several documents that convinced him. What were they and where are they now? Perhaps like the Clement letter, they have been disappeared. An academic somewhere must be able to trace his source. Of course he was a member of the Royal Society, which suggests he was a Freemasons and he lived many years on the continent and spoke French. Does this confirm that the Templars knew the truth which was passed onto the high initiates in Freemasonry? Remember the 27th Degree of the Freemason's states *'The importance of denial of the cross!'* Or is it possible he could have studied the documents in St. Sulpice, the same ones Canon Lilley saw that convinced him the crucifixion was a fraud?

There is a strange transition between the martyrdom of the Galilean's followers to that of the Christians. We have this description of the martyrdom of the Sicarii in Egypt after the fall of Masada around AD 73:

'Subjected to every form of torture and bodily suffering that could be thought of, for the one purpose of making them acknowledge Caesar as their lord, not a man gave in or came near to saying it, but rising above the strongest compulsion

they all maintained their resolve, and it seemed as if their bodies felt no pain and their souls were almost exultant as they met the tortures and the flames.' (Josephus, War 23)

Refusing to accept Caesar as a God or worship any of the other Roman gods is exactly what the Christian Martyrs are accused of, just forty years later. The Christians were called atheists because they would not worship the Roman Gods and were sent to death and mutilation in the arena. The same God, the same crime, the same punishment, but totally opposed ideologies: one group, the followers of the Galilean who were rebellious assassins, the others, peace-loving followers of Jesus. Perhaps to the Roman mind they could not distinguish between these two sects who followed the same single Jewish God, the same Holy book, and both refused to pay homage to the Roman pantheon of Gods. It almost looks like there could have been a real confusion between the two groups. A confusion exploited by later Christian forgers. But research into the mixing up of these two sects, as suggested by Gibbon, must be undertaken. And crucial to this research must be the name of Judas the Galilean's sect, because Josephus always says the 'fourth philosophy of the Galilean'. It cannot be that mouthful, it must have had a name and I have a strong suspicion that the astonishing answer is revealed here when Paul is bought to trial.

"We have found this man to be a troublemaker, stirring up riots among the Jews all over the world. He is a ringleader of the Nazarene sect and even tried to desecrate the temple; so we seized him. (Acts 24:5)

And Paul answers:

"They cannot prove to you the charges they are now making against me. However, I admit that I worship the God of our ancestors as a follower of the Way, which they call a sect. I believe everything that is in accordance with the Law and that is written in the Prophets." (Acts 24:14)

So Paul says he belongs to a sect called *'The Way'* who obey the law, but denies he belongs to the sect of *'troublemakers, stirring up riots among the Jews all over the world.'* The Nazarene sect!

This strongly suggests Judas' *'troublemaking'* sect was called the *'Nazarenes'* whereas Jesus sect was called *'The Way.'* As Paul said they *'both worship the God of our ancestors'*, but they are different sects. I am almost certain that Nazarene was initially introduced into Jesus name to deliberately confuse the two sects and it looks like Prof. Eisenman nearly came to the same conclusion:

'In Jesus' case, Nazoraean and Galilean would both appear to be esotericisms referring to the 'Messianic' or 'Zealot' movement. [Zealot being Judas the Galilean followers] Nazareth if it existed at all, may have been a little village not far from Sepphoris. Nazareth may have sprung into life to meet a later need. Where Judas the Galilean is concerned....' (Eisenman – James the brother..)

He is tantalizing close to my conclusions but veers of in a different direction.

I should add that, *'The Way'* is the term Pythagoras used for his philosophy, which fits perfectly into my belief that the ideas and secret initiations that Pythagoras members went through are exactly what Jesus *'the Hierophant'* was teaching.

Finally there is one thing that we cannot accept. Remember Suetonius and the Bible mention the expulsion of the Jews from Rome:

'After this Paul left Athens and went to Corinth. There he fund a Jew named Aquila, a native of Pontus, who had recently come from Italy with his wife Priscilla, because Claudius had ordered all Jews to leave Rome.' (Acts 18:1-2)

And from Suetonius.

'Since the Jews constantly made disturbances at the instigation of Chrestus, he [the Emperor Claudius] expelled them from Rome.'

So why is this major Jewish event not in the books of Josephus? It happened around 49 AD, right in the middle of his War book and Jews must have been arriving back in Judea after the event. This must have been in Josephus but obviously it must have told us who this important Jewish rebel, Chrestus was.

But an even more revealing omission is that, Josephus wrote his War book in Rome in AD 75. He often diverts his story from Israel to Rome, when Jews are involved. So I find it absolutely impossible to believe that he never mentions the Great Fire of Rome or the persecution of the Jews who were responsible; even though he does mention several minor misdemeanors by Jews in Rome. He *must* have written something about such a massive event that destroyed seventy percent of the city and was blamed on followers of a Jew (whoever you believe it was, Jesus or Judas) and led to the persecution of hundreds of them. Not only that but it is just two years before the actual war and must have influenced in some way the Jewish fighters. It is like writing a book on the US invasion of Afghanistan and not mentioning the 9/11 'Twin Towers' attack.

The Great Fire happened just seven years *before* he arrived in Rome and sat down to write, so they must have still been rebuilding parts of the city all around him. And it is not that he does not mention Nero, he writes quite a bit about him. But the Great Fire – nothing.

This leaves us with just three possible scenarios. Either, this Jewish event in Rome somehow slipped his memory and he forgot to mention it in either book. Or he didn't think it was important enough to mention. Or he did mention it and it was cut out for some reason. Surely all logic tells us it was there but was cut out. Why? The only possible reason was that it contradicted some aspect of the biblical story. And ask yourself in what way could Josephus' account of the Great Fire of Rome, contradict the Gospel story? Can you come up with any other answer than the obvious?

One other omission I must mention. When I realized the date of Jesus death was AD 38, I went back over all my books to see if there were any clues to that date. Opening Tacitus' *'Annals of Imperial Rome'* I skipped to the death of Tiberius in AD 37, turned the page expecting AD 38 but found this in brackets.

[The manuscript breaks off at the death of Tiberius, and Tacitus' description of the four years reign of the unbalanced Caligula is lost]

How the hell did that happen? I can just imagine a line of monks opening copies of 'Annals' and tearing out the offending seven pages and tossing them in the fire. The mind boggles.

Here is a great illuminated text from the Latin version of the 'War' book with Josephus holding open his work and a monk copying (or is it doctoring) it for posterity. What I want to know is what did the Monk do with the original?

I have been saving one very crucial piece of information for those who still doubt the theory. It happened at the first Ecumenical Council, which occurred in AD 325 in the city of Nicaea. The Church fathers produced the Nicene Creed, which, as mentioned, is now central to all forms of Christianity. The creed starts with:

1. We believe in one God,
2. the Father, the sum of all powers,

And continues with: (numbered for convenience)

16. he came down
17. and became flesh
18. and became human.
19. and suffered death
20. and rose again the third day

Nothing that surprising in this is there? But wait for it: fifty years later in Constantinople in AD 381 at the second Ecumenical Council certain changes were made to the creed; changes, which must have been important for them to be added to the original creed. Did I say important I mean extraordinarily important! (In bold are these additions)

16. he came down *from the air-and-sky*
17. and became flesh
18. *from the Holy Spirit and Mary the Virgin*
19. and became human.
20. *He was crucified for us under Pontius Pilate*
21. and suffered death **and was buried**
22. and rose again the third day *as written*

So there you have it, in AD 381, some 350 years after the events; and at exactly the same time Crucifixion paintings began to appear, the Crucifixion of Jesus by Pilate suddenly became a new matter of faith.

That Jesus was the Son of God should be a matter of faith. Belief in the resurrection from death should be a matter of faith. That Jesus turned water into wine is a matter of faith. But Pilate crucifying Jesus is not a matter of faith! It is either a historical fact or it is not a fact. There is only one possible conclusion to draw from this and that is, that it was clearly not accepted as a fact by many people and therefore had to be forced on them as a matter of faith. Anyone who did not accept the Nicene Creed would be excommunicated and, right up to the Middle Ages could be burnt to death as a heretic, if they were lucky. Can you imagine what torture they would devise if you dared to suggest Jesus did not die on the cross? I have read some sickening things in my research, which I don't want to inflict on you, as they have kept me awake at night. Remember Priscillian, the very first supposed heretic, was killed by the Church of Rome just four years after the second Ecumenical Council announced that, 'Jesus crucified by Pilate' was a matter of faith. After over a thousand years of persecution, I would be very surprised to find anyone who knows, or believes that, Pontius Pilate did not crucify Jesus.

There are things I am still not sure about like, why John the Baptist seems to play such an important part in esoteric thinking or who exactly was Joseph of Arimathea who appears so frequently in Holy Grail stories. But what I feel I have proven is that the French esoteric circles are right to believe Jesus was alive after Pilate left Judea clearly making it impossible for Pontius Pilate to have crucified him. And that Judas the Galilean impregnated his wife not much earlier than AD 20 and not much later that AD 34 to produce a son Menachem. So his unreported death must have been between these dates, or in other words during the time when Pilate was in Judea.

I have also proven that huge chunks about Judas the Galilean have been cut from Josephus's *War* book as Josephus states quite clearly later in the book that he has *'recorded earlier'* the Galilean's exploits when in fact it is no longer there. And in the *Antiquities* book he again states about the exploits of the Galilean, *'as we have shown in a foregoing book'*, but, which is again no longer there. If there was a need to cut much of Judas out of the book, then there must have been some revealing connection between the story of Jesus and the story of Judas the Galilean, something that questions the events in the Bible and clearly the Crucifixion switch is the only likely candidate.

In the first century while the people of Israel were being decimated by the Roman army, the people of Provence clearly knew all of these findings, from the incoming Jews especially the beloved family from Bethany, which is why they needed to be wiped out in a crusade followed by the Spanish Inquision.

But Mary Magdalene who Jesus kissed and called the blessed one, the woman who knew the all, the disciple of disciples, the local population clearly took her to their hearts as Notre Dame (our lady) and they were prepared to die rather than renounce her teachings. She must have been something special to have had such an influence on the whole region. Like Jesus, they clearly loved her.

THE END

Julian Doyle takes the knee in memory of Mary Magdalene
outside the cathedral of Notre Dame they stole from her.
Photo. Sukanya Panyamat

ABOUT THE AUTHOR

JULIAN DOYLE is one of the world's most versatile filmmakers. He has written and directed his own films, and edited, photographed and created Fx on others. He is most famous for editing the Monty Python Films and shooting the Fxs for Terry Gilliam's movies 'TimeBandits and 'Brazil', which he also edited.

He has written and directed three feature films. 'Love Potion' about a drug rehabilitation centre, described as *'Hitchcockian'*. 'Chemical Wedding' featuring Simon Callow about the outrageous British occultist, Aleister Crowley and described by one American reviewer as *'Thoroughly entertaining although at times you wonder if the film makers have not lost all there senses'*. He has also directed award winning pop videos such as Kate Bush's 'CloudBusting' featuring Donald Sutherland and Iron Maiden's 'Play With Madness'.

He recently wrote and directed the play 'Twilight of the Gods' investigating the tumultuous relationship between Richard Wagner and Friedrich Nietzsche and described by 'Philosophy Today' as *'Masterful!'* Python's, Terry Jones has described Julian as an original Polymath.

Julian was born in London and started life in the slums of Paddington. His Irish father, Bob, was one of the youngest members of the International Brigade that went to fight against Franco's invasion of democratic Spain. His mother, Lola, was born in Spain of an Asturian miner who died early of silicosis. She was thereafter brought up in a Catholic orphanage in Oviedo.

Julian started his education at St. Saviours, a church primary school. He went on to Haverstock secondary school, one of the first comprehensive schools in England. His first job was as a junior technician to Professor Peter Medawar's team, who won the Nobel Prize soon after Julian's arrival. Not that he claims any credit for that. At night school he passed his 'A' level exams and took a Zoology degree at London University. After a year at the Institute of Education, he taught biology before going to the London Film School. On leaving he started a film company with other students. Besides film making, Julian is well known for his Master-classes in Film Directing.

While still at school, Julian had a daughter, Margarita who was brought up in the family. He then had two further children, Jud and Jessie.

Clearly, Julian Doyle is a very naughty boy!

ALSO BY JULIAN DOYLE

THE GOSPEL ACCORDING TO MONTY PYTHON

Who was the real Brian?
Who was the real Jesus?
Who was the real Bishop of
Southwark?
Did the Romans build the
Jerusalem Aqueduct?
Were the Magi wise?
Was Brian's father Nortius
Maximus, and
Were the Peoples Front of
Judea, really splitters?

All the crucial issues this book dares to confront.

With a FOREWORD by TERRY JONES

And a BACKWORD by MICHAEL PALIN

Amazon US   https://www.amazon.com/dp/1981903569
Amazon UK   https://www.amazon.co.uk/dp/1981903569